RESTORATION OF CLASS SOCIETY IN RUSSIA?

Restoration of Class Society in Russia?

Edited by

JOUKO NIKULA

Routledge
Taylor & Francis Group
LONDON AND NEW YORK

First published 2002 by Ashgate Publishing

Reissued 2019 by Routledge
2 Park Square, Milton Park, Abingdon, Oxon, OXl 4 4RN
52 Vanderbilt Avenue, New York, NY 10017

Routledge is an imprint of the Taylor & Francis Group, an informa business

Copyright © Jouko Nikula 2002

All rights reserved. No part of this book may be reprinted or reproduced or utilised in any form or by any electronic, mechanical, or other means, now known or hereafter invented, including photocopying and recording, or in any information storage or retrieval system, without permission in writing from the publishers.

Notice:
Product or corporate names may be trademarks or registered trademarks, and are used only for identification and explanation without intent to infringe.

Publisher's Note
The publisher has gone to great lengths to ensure the quality of this reprint but points out that some imperfections in the original copies may be apparent.

Disclaimer
The publisher has made every effort to trace copyright holders and welcomes correspondence from those they have been unable to contact.

A Library of Congress record exists under LC control number:

ISBN 13: 978-1-138-72559-1 (hbk)
ISBN 13: 978-1-138-72553-9 (pbk)
ISBN 13: 978-1-315-19182-9 (ebk)

Contents

Notes on Contributors

Raimo Blom, Professor of Sociology at the University of Tampere. Speciality: class, social consciousness, social integration.

Michail Chernish, Senior Researcher at the Institute of Sociology, Russian Academy of Sciences. Speciality: social mobility, values and life style.

Harri Melin, Professor of Sociology at the University of Tampere. Speciality: class structure, managerial structures and labour process in Soviet Union and Russia.

Jouko Nikula, Researcher at the Finnish Centre for Russian and East European Studies, Helsinki. Speciality: position of working class in post-socialist society, rural transformation.

Introduction

Jouko Nikula

It is no great exaggeration to say that the short history of modern Russia is condensed into two August dates: 19 August 1991, when the world watched the Soviet Union in its death throes, and 17 August 1998, when the country's economy collapsed. In 1991 President Yeltsin emerged as a national hero when he suppressed the coup d'état: he gained huge popularity as a representative of the new, democratic Russia, committed to the best principles of 'modern' western societies. Seven years on, Yeltsin was seen as the ultimate cause of all the country's social, economic and political problems and an obstacle to necessary reform. Among the countries of social transformation, Russia has been one of the most contradictory and troubled nations. Economic reform has resulted in a sharp decline in production and GDP (dropping by 38% between 1991 and 1996) as well as in income levels to the extent that it is justified to say that Russia is 'essentially a non-monetary society' (Clarke 1997).

The list of unintended 'achievements' in the Russian reform is quite exhausting. Instead of having a parliamentary democracy with a normal division of executive and legislative powers, the country has seen the development of a system of non-coordinated institutions, each competing for power and money. The lack of social and system integration is highlighted by the complete lack of any integrating ideology. Instead, there is intense competition over the hegemonic 'programme for Russia's future development' – whether that is based on past grandeur, military might, religious values or market liberalism. This situation has nurtured practices of favouritism and corruption and all-embracing suspicion and hostility, which in turn have eroded the fragile legitimacy of the political and economic leaders in the country.

The Russian mode of transformation shows some similarities with other post-socialist countries, but also several striking particularities that have not been visible in any other country. The basic ideology of Russian reform policy was exactly the same IMF orthodoxy as in all other post-socialist countries: liberalization, stabilization, privatization, restructuration. As in other countries, the lifting of price controls immediately brought galloping inflation. However, unlike Estonia or the Czech Republic, the Russian government failed to introduce a solid anti-inflationary programme, but instead opted to print more money and to take various contradictory fiscal policy decisions. These have led to a sharp increase in prices, a shortage of cash for enterprises, causing debt problems and increased barter and other non-monetary types of transaction.

The Russian approach to privatization has been widely reported and analysed. 'Shock privatization' gave power to insiders in the firm and created a new stratum of wealthy businesspeople who enjoyed state protection. Two things were particularly important in this process: first, the close relationship between the political elite and the new economic elite, and second, the development of clear economic-political power blocs on the basis of these relationships. These blocs continued to expand and gain influence until the economic crash in late 1998, but they still continue to exert a destabilizing influence on government policies. Another major factor behind the instability and lack of coordination is the marginal role that Parliament plays in the political decision-making process, in comparison with that of the Duma and the Federation Council.

The most peculiar deviance is the development in the spheres of production and the labour market. It was widely expected that unemployment would soar in Russia, given the key role that the state sector and arms production traditionally played in the national economy. The country had experimented with various managerial strategies, from soviets and one-man management and adjoining versions of soviet-Taylorism to work brigades and team-working. None of these were able to solve the basic problems of the Soviet economy, its dependence on central planning organs and the problems of shortage and waste. These problems created relations of interdependence between planning authorities and directors, managers and workers, fuelled by bribes and blat. It was expected that all of this would be wiped out with privatization, which would force businesses to face hard budget constraints. Russia was a top-ranking pupil of market economy at least in terms of the speed it was moving ahead with privatization, though in other spheres its success was less convincing. Now, almost ten years on, questions are being asked about the goals of the privatization programme: was it just a magnificent and well-planned seizure of public property, or an honest attempt to create people's capitalism?

According to western observers the main objective for the directors of the former state companies was simply to safeguard their own power positions, not ownership as such. In principle the insider privatization scheme meant that employees were to become owners as well, in practice they got very little at all. In many spheres the immediate result of privatization was a rapid decline in production, as no investments were made to renew machinery or infrastructure.

However, the sharp decline in production and the financial difficulties that hit many companies did not result in any dramatic increase in unemployment: between 1992–1995/96, the unemployment rate remained at around 2–5 per cent. The unemployment figures did not begin to rise until after 1997, reaching 17–20 per cent of the labour force. All these figures are official numbers; it is likely that the true figures are twice as high. The explanation for this Russian miracle of low unemployment lies in increasing oil revenues and in wage arrears, which have affected all sectors of the economy and both the state and private sector. Some observers put the blame for wage arrears on the country's tight monetary policy, others on underdeveloped controls of fiscal policy, others still saw it as a way of avoiding the social tensions that would follow with higher unemployment. Whatever the true reason, wage arrears represented a heavier burden for those segments of the labour force that did not possess strong power resources either for competitiveness in their employment sector or for skills. The groups to suffer most were clerical workers in the state sector and unskilled labourers. Neither had very much choice: they either had to accept being paid late or face losing their job (Gimpelson 1999).

The Relevance of Class in Modern Russia

The developments in the economy on the one hand and in the ideological and political system on the other, have produced a diverging pattern of class system in Russian society. Economic failures have resulted in a sharp increase in poverty and marginalization, at the same time as the number of nouveaux-riches has slowly but steadily grown. Expectations of a rapid formation of middle classes were dashed by the autumn crisis of 1998. Nevertheless there are sharp divisions between social groups according to levels of income and general well-being and also in labour market positions. Despite the rapid growth of poverty and the social divisions, there are very few social organizations representing the interests of any of these groups. In this sense one may argue that social classes do not exist in Russia; there are only social strata that differ from one another with respect to their incomes or other indicators of market capacities.

Opinion polls conducted in Russia in the 1990s draw very a consistent picture of the 'mental climate' in the country: that picture is dominated by feelings of anomie, helplessness and a sense of being an innocent victim in the power play of competing political and economic elites. Even though the Yeltsin government put an end to the supremacy of the Communist Party, the mushrooming of new parties and organizations has not led to a rebirth of civil society or a strengthening of civic democracy. Quite the contrary: the myriad of splinter-parties and their political intrigues and log-rolling has caused the 'masses' to retreat into privacy. In their everyday life, coping with the economic hardship is more important than the political wrangling that goes on in Parliament. In a sense it is legitimate to speak about at least a two-layered society, one that people visit as citizens and subjects of the state and the other, in which people actually live their lives. In their 'real life', relations with relatives, friends and colleagues from work are most important of all, because much of their livelihood is dependent on these relations, which are based on reciprocity.

As Simon Clarke (1996) has noted, the workplace was 'a second home' for people during the Soviet era: the labour collective was very important both for workers and for management, for workers as a provider of benefits and services and for management as a source of labour and support in struggles over resources. The trade union had little relevance for workers as a channel of interest representation, serving as it did mainly as a 'rubber-stamp' for the interests of management. A large number of new unions have entered the field since the collapse of socialism, but still the old union has most members and influence. The new unions have remained quite small and powerless, defending the interests of the economic branch rather than those of the workers in the branch. Russia has seen a number of strikes during the past couple of years, organized mainly by miners and teachers. Many of these have been wildcat strikes, organized without the unions' consent, and they have been chiefly aimed at resolving the problem of wage arrears.

There is good reason to argue then that there are no classes in Russia: there are no class organizations in the country and there is no class action. Equally, one can argue that western theories of class, such as those by E.O. Wright or John Goldthorpe that are based on certain assumptions on the type and nature of the organization of work and forms of ownership and livelihood, are of very limited use in the analysis and explanation of post-socialist countries overall and Russia in particular.

There are in fact several variations of theories that deny the relevance of class analysis in the post-socialist context of Russia. One of them is the theory which says there are no classes in Russia, but only strata that differ from one another on the basis of income, education and way of life or consumption patterns (see Radayev 1998, Zaslavskaya 1997). Another theory places the emphasis on sources of income, whether official, semi-legal or alegal or illegal: here strata are constructed on the basis of different types of 'portfolios' of various sources of income (see Piirainen 1996, Rose et al. 1998). As in other stratification theories, the main problem here is the arbitrary definition of boundaries between strata. On the other hand, it allows us to define an infinite number of subgroups without any theoretical justification.

Given the 'essentially non-monetary nature of society', the income-based definition of classes is particularly poorly suited to the case of Russia: incomes will only cover a small proportion of people's actual resources. The distribution of incomes between occupational groups in post-socialist Russia also blurs the boundaries of social groups so that many working class occupations are clearly in a better position than many white-collar, 'middle class' occupations such as teachers, nurses, lower managers, etc.

Another, more radical strand of theories states bluntly that modern social theories are unable to understand, let alone explain, the Russian reality.

Russian society, it is argued, is a product of so complex historical, cultural and religious traditions that the only way it can be understood is by theories of cultural history or other methods of human sciences. This argument is based on the view that Russia is 'another kind of civilization', not Asian, nor European, but Russian. Advocates seek justification for this from folk traditions, a long imperial legacy, Orthodox religion, literature, from the mixture of Tsarism and Bolshevism, etc. We maintain that this thinking is merely a mystification of Russia on one level and a means of struggle for hegemony in the field of Russian studies. Russia has not been a 'typical' country in any period of her development, but it has followed the path of 'modernization'.

The socialist period marked the end of the peasantist nature of Russian society: rapid urbanization and 'forced' industrialization followed from the 1930s through to the 1960s. Talk about an 'ultimately peasantist society', whether in habits or culture, is therefore a gross exaggeration. The Soviet Union did not uproot the religious traditions and habits of Russians, but nor was the church a haven of resistance or dissidence as in Poland. In fact the church supported the regime in many ways. Imperial traditions are more a political or ideological tool than an all-pervasive and effecting part of reality.

What we have said above does not mean that history or tradition or culture plays no role in the analysis of Russian society; they do. However, their role is to serve as an element of explanation, as a context rather than as the explanation in itself or as a starting point and ending point.

In our view contemporary Russia is an industrial society that carries the same characteristics as any other industrial society. Cultural and historical aspects can partly explain its specificities and exceptions. Modern Russia is not a capitalist society, nor is it a 'typical' post-socialist society: indeed there is no such thing as a typical capitalist or post-socialist society, there are only different variants of both forms. However, modern Russia certainly is a class society, and it bears a striking similarity to societies of early capitalism during the era of original accumulation. These societies were characterized by a small number of very rich businessmen and a large body of 'free' labour who had no social or political organization to articulate their interests. True, Russian society is not a case of early pure capitalist society in the sense that economic power is not in the hands of a few industrialists, but in the hands of a limited number of industrial oligarchies. On the other hand, the collapse of socialism did not result in the rapid growth of middle classes, but in a sharp increase in the number of poor people, while maintaining a large segment of the working class that existed during socialism. In a sense this process has polarized the social structure: at the top there is a small group of industrial and commercial capitalists, together with the nouveaux-riches, born out of political capital or speculative capital. At the bottom there are various layers of workers and marginalized groups who differ in terms of their level of income, skills and sources of income.

This book describes and analyses the social development of Russia during the 1990s on the basis of the analytical principle of the scope logic of class analysis (Blom et al. 1992), in which the accent is on the different levels of class analysis. According to this methodological principle the description of class positions is merely a starting point that has to be followed by a number of other steps. The description of class positions is followed by an analysis of work and reproduction situations, which is then followed by an analysis of the social and political organization of social groups. Drawing on the information accumulated in the previous stages, the two final steps are the analysis of social groups in relation to the state and the redefinition of the class structure.

This methodological solution strives to resolve the dilemmas and anomalies of structure and action by emphasizing the relevance and importance of such areas as work situation, reproduction and social organization and action in understanding the features of social structure.

The main question we address in this book is as follows: Can Russia be described as a market and a class society and if so, on what grounds? From this vantage point the contributors cast a critical view on standard ways of understanding the social structure of present-day Russia, either as a predominantly middle-class society or as an amorphous mass society.

The aim of this book is to further our understanding of a transition society through an in-depth analysis of its structures, particularly its social structure. The data available allow us to reconstitute the process of structural change in these societies and provide ample material for us to test the applicability of various theories for the analysis of social transition. The accent in the structural analysis will be on the processes of class becoming and formation, reproduction conditions, integration strategies, social mobility and cultural predispositions.

The Theme

We start our analysis from the question of classes: how have the class structure, class situations and class processes developed since the early 1990s? Is a specific kind of mobility pattern developing in Russia and if so, what are its main characteristics? As noted above, our methodological principle here is the scope logic analysis of class structure, which means that we reject the approach that is based on counting the sizes – relative or absolute – of different class groups or strata. As Markku Kivinen (1998, 106) notes: *'In fact class analysis is a complex entity involving different conceptual levels and strategies of research. The basic difference is the difference between class position and class situation'*. More concretely, a difference has to be made between position in the relations of ownership and power and situation in reproduction, incomes, education or labour market. In the current discussion on class theory, there is a strong line of argument in favour of the gradual erosion of class differences and the general dispersion of classes due to the declining relevance of work in peoples' life, changing patterns of ownership, etc. On the surface then, post-socialist countries would seem to be in the vanguard of this process, but as Kivinen (1998, 106) notes, it is wholly misleading to view these countries as some kind of status-bazaars. On the contrary, an entirely new set of processes is now unfolding in Russia and other post-socialist countries, reconstructing the class structure. These processes include the rebirth of the class of owners, inflation of former social and cultural capitals and modifications in managerial structures. In addition, one must not forget that past lives are still with us today, i.e. that structures and practices from the socialist period have by no means lost all their relevance but continue to modify the emergent structures. Therefore, neither the process of the growth of middle classes nor the process of proletarianization are adequate characterizations of the changing class structure.

These same processes are also impacting the patterns of social mobility, which in the past was restricted and politically controlled. The end of community party power and central planning has not meant a decisive shift towards an 'open society', which has been the main argument of modernization theory. Many studies in post-socialist countries have shown that for the majority of the population, the main trend has been a lowering of social status with the disintegration of systems of welfare and employment. The history of Soviet society which included industrialization, collectivization, purges and totalitarian mobilization 'produced' extensive mobility. As Chernish notes in this volume 'High social mobility has been regarded by Russian citizens as a major achievement of Russian, formerly Soviet society in the twentieth century, equality and chances of upward mobility came to be one of the most prominent ideals'.

This consisted of four, interrelated aspects of mobility: mobility of status, mobility of power, territorial mobility and mobility to better living standards. The prerequisites for these forms of mobility were hard work, diligence, loyalty to the country and Party. Chernish goes on to argue that 'The Soviet dream was in many respects similar to the American one' and indeed one can see core elements of the Fordist model of 'good life', where hard work and devotion to key values of American society were the pathways to a higher social position. How about today, what are the matters on which social mobility is seen to be dependent, and what are the main patterns of mobility in Russia? Due to the specific nature of the relation between economy and politics in the Soviet Union, the traditional, western-type mobility theory does not work in the Russian context. The late-Soviet period in the late 1960s and early

1970s provided very good chances for upward mobility for the post-war generation.

The last decade of Soviet power saw a sharp decline in mobility rates as a result of the general decline of the economy and production. Nowadays the mobility patterns are approximating those seen in the 'west', with well-educated upper white-collar employees in the private sector holding on to their prospects for advancement, while the majority of blue-collar workers and lower white-collar employees and 'specialists' in the state sector face a dead-end. The transition from socialism towards the market economy has rendered many success factors futile, while giving more emphasis to entirely new ones. The factors that have lost their importance include those that were revered during socialism: hard work, education, law abidance, appropriate political views or natural intellect. Rich parents, risk-taking and good connections are now seen as most important for success. So, the Soviet version of the American dream has died and been replaced by an image of Las Vegas society, where only the quick-witted win. On a structural level this implies a bipartite development: on the one hand there is a small number of very wealthy and powerful people, on the other hand there is a large group of people whose social position is declining on all criteria. This means that there is no strong tendency for the middle classes to grow, but at least at the time of the study (autumn 1998) their ranks were dwindling.

As in many other post-socialist countries, the transition in Russia has created sharp social inequalities in terms of income, employment and general standards of living. One of the reasons for this is that following the collapse of socialism, many countries believed, in the spirit of monetarist ultra-liberalism, that the dismantling of the state and state-sponsored social responsibilities (such as social benefits and subsidies) was a key precondition for successful transition to market economy. In Russia the struggle over previously state-owned resources led to a dual result: on the one hand to a weak state and to the formation of strong private industrial-financial interest groups, and on the other hand to the blurring of the boundary line between public (state) and private.

In Russia the weak state appears in the shape of a poor state which is unable to pay decent wages, which encourages bribery, deters the development of social security, which in turns forces people to rely on social networks. How, then, are people coping in a society which is virtually a non-monetary society? What is the role of social networks, second jobs or plot-farming which have been seen as fundamentally important preconditions for survival? Simon Clarke and his colleagues have argued that there are no specific survival strategies and that those things that have been thought to be crucial, are crucial only in a limited sense. However, there are also 'winners' in transition, and to be a winner one has to meet certain criteria: to occupy a managerial position, to live in the capital area and to be well educated. But these winners only represent a very small minority and between them and those who can be regarded as poor, there is a wide range of different statuses. A significant part of the economy is geared to the informal sector, an area where double wages and no taxes are paid, where reciprocal relations of exchange are important and which is out of state control and regulation. All these phenomena are clear symptoms of the lack of confidence in the state and its institutions.

The Data

Our aim is to present an all-inclusive sociological analysis of Russian society on the basis of two nationwide surveys. In the late 1980s the Finnish Class Project and a team of sociologists from the Institute of Sociology at the Soviet Academy of Sciences initiated a couple of projects aiming to compare the social structures of Finland and the Soviet Union. These two projects met on a regular basis to discuss and agree upon the joint questionnaire and principles of sampling. The results were not very encouraging: while the Finnish team created a standard, representative sample from Finland (see Nikula 1989), the Soviet team produced two or three samples from different areas, including Voronezh, Alma Ata and Nishni-Tagil. The argument was that these were 'normal' areas in the Soviet context, representing 'typical areas' where the selection of respondents was based on a division between industries, not individuals or households.

A more reliable data set from the former Soviet Union was collected in spring 1991 by the Soviet Academy of Sciences in collaboration with the International Project on Social Structure and Social Consciousness, headed by professor Erik Olin Wright. This sample, comprising 2600 persons, was collected in the form of personal interviews from the European side of the Russian Federation. The data are reliable in most respects, for instance in terms of divisions according to region, gender, age, occupation and economic branch. Naturally the data do not represent the whole of the former Soviet Union, but only the European part of the country. That leaves some potentially important areas uncovered, but for the purposes of the present study that does not represent any major flaw since the areas of Far East are predominantly less industrialized. The data also do not cover centres of military production such as Samara or major coal-mining areas. It is also noteworthy that the data only cover the Russian Federation and not other republics, which means that we cannot look at differences between the republics in terms of industrial structure, etc. The main data base for this study was collected immediately after the August crisis in October-November 1998. The sample design was based on the assumption that the overall sample should comprise about 1 600 households or 3000 respondents. The basis of the sample, the so-called primary sampling unit (PSU) was *rayon* because *rayons* are comparatively small and fairly well described in the statistical and other literature, and data on *rayons* are not classified. Thirdly, the number of *rayons* in the Russian Federation is close to 2800. The sample design was based on the data of the 1989 All-Russia Census conducted by the State Committee of Statistics and the MicroCensus of 1994. To counter possible bias, the latest update of the data (1996) by the State Committee of Statistics was used.

Chapter 1

Towards a Working Class Society: the Russian Class Structure in the 1990s

Harri Melin

Introduction

For many Western commentators Russian society appears as something of an enigma that is virtually impossible to capture in a rigorous sociological analysis. It is true of course that Russia is very different from most European countries, and during the momentous changes of the past decade or so it has been very difficult to predict the future path of social change. The old system of state socialism has collapsed and given way to a peculiar set of capitalist social relations. On the other hand, Russia today may be described as a social formation that comprises elements of emergent capitalism combined with substantial remnants of the old Soviet system (see Simon 1999). The pace of change has at once been extremely rapid and very slow.

So does Russia today qualify as a modern society; does it meet the relevant criteria in terms of democracy, private property, market economy, civil society, and wage labour? In many respects the answer has to be no. Russia is a constitutional republic in which all the formal state institutions are in place, but it is quite clear that Russia cannot be described as a democratic society. Its party system and parliamentarism in general are highly unstable. The division of power in today's Russian state is a peculiar mixture of 'Tsarism' and modernity. There are many rival political coalitions, the country has a new constitution, and democratically elected political institutions are also in place.

Although the means of production are not owned by the state, the links between the state and the economy remain tight. Politicians are important economic actors, and the economic elite in the country is an influential political actor. Private business is still in many ways highly dependent on the state. Although banks are highly influential and powerful actors, money remains in a secondary role compared to non-monetary transactions. Combine with all this the fact that the Russian economy is integrated into the global economy chiefly through its role as a producer of raw materials, and it becomes clear why levels of productivity in the country are so very low. Profits are generated not through surplus value, but through trade and exchange (see Clarke 1999).

The Russian economy has by now been largely privatized. Its markets are in place, including a labour market where unemployment currently stands at almost 20 per cent. There is also an established banking system, and the value of the currency is determined on the marketplace. However, even these features do not warrant the description of Russia as a modern market economy or a market society as it would be understood in Europe. As yet there have been no deep-going social transitions (cf. Sutela 1998).

Russian society is in a state of constant flux, but no one really knows where the country is heading or at what speed. Some of the former Soviet republics, most notably the Baltic states, have set the explicit target of joining the European Union and NATO. But otherwise, the future of Russia is very much open.

The social changes that are sweeping across this vast country are having many and varied impacts on people's everyday life and living conditions. The aim of the discussion below is to take a closer look at the social distinctions prevailing in today's Russia. Our chief concern is with this one question: How has the social structure in Russia changed during the past decade? The discussion is grounded in class analysis: the focus is on the changes that have happened in the Russian class structure during the 1990s.

The Changing Class Structure

The Soviet Union was a class society. There were several, even contradictory theories of the nature and the structure of Soviet society. The three main interpretations about the foundations of Soviet class structure were:

- the official theory of class relations in socialism
- conceptions based on theories of power
- socialism as a special form of exploitation (see Melin 1996, 31)

According to the official understanding there were two social classes in the Soviet Union: first, the industrial working class and second, peasants on collective farms. In addition, there was the social stratum made up by the intelligentsia. The official theory also had it that there were no conflicts of interest between the two classes, but they were both committed to the joint project of building socialist society under the guidance of the Communist Party.

The communist project in the Soviet Union lasted more than 70 years. During this period what was an essentially agrarian society transformed within the space of no more than 20 years into an industrial society. The structural changes implied by this transformation also impacted the Soviet class structure. Although the official view remained that there were just the two classes in society, there was in fact a tendency for the middle classes to gain more and more ground (bearing in mind, of course, that in the Soviet context we cannot refer to the middle class in the same sense as in capitalist countries), but the underlying social processes were quite similar.

Once transformed into an industrial society, the Soviet Union shared many structures and social positions that were based on industrial organizations in common with those we see in capitalist countries. As technological development continued to make the economic system more and more complex, the proportion of the highly educated strata continued to grow and the numbers of unskilled labourers declined. In 1939, less than 20 per cent of the economically active population in the Soviet Union occupied white-collar (non-manual) positions, in 1979 the figure was over 35 per cent (Melin 1996, 50).

Sociological class theory is divided into two main lines of argumentation, which are based on the Marxist and the Weberian tradition. Marxist theory explains class relations by reference to ownership relations, Weberian theory refers to market positions. In the Soviet Union class position was determined neither on the basis of ownership nor on the basis of markets. The Soviet class structure was essentially a political and economic construct. In the Soviet case we may also speak about strata relations based on differences in the nature of work rather than about dichotomous class relations.

Some commentators have said that Soviet society was divided into two classes, viz. the dominant power elite (new class, nomenklatura) and the exploited working class (e.g. Djilas 1957). These theories suggest, in essence, that the state socialist system was simply a new form of class rule (oppression). Some have also calculated the size of this 'new class': it has been suggested that in the early 1980s, this ruling class accounted for about one per cent of the entire population (Melin 1996, 68).

To me this concept does not provide a valid analysis of social reality in the former Soviet Union. There was not only one ruling elite, but several rival elites in the Soviet Union. There was also much social mobility between the elites. These theories of the new class are essentially political constructs rather than based on any serious sociological analysis of concrete society.

The modernization of Russia started towards the end of the nineteenth century as capitalist social relations began to take over from the former feudal social relations. This gave rise to increased social mobility. There was also much social mobility in the former Soviet Union. During certain historical periods this mobility was largely determined by political events. The first such period came after the revolution in the early 1920s when the old political and economic elite was destroyed and a new social order created. There were no end of empty positions that had to be filled. The second wave of mobility came with industrialization and Stalin's purges. During these years virtually the whole regime was annihilated and replaced: politicians, managers and the military all had to go. Fresh forces were promoted into important social positions.

The third wave of high social mobility came with the era of reconstruction after World War II. Then, in the 1960s, the mobility pattern shifted and began to follow the same line as in Western countries. At that time the main reason behind upward mobility was education and new qualifications. Overall social mobility during the last two decades of the Soviet era remained at a much lower level than during earlier periods: stagnation gained ground, making the structures of society far more rigid than before.

High levels of social mobility are indicative of a certain openness in the social order. In the Soviet Union, people could reach high positions of political or economic authority from virtually any kind of starting point. Therefore the nomenklatura, for instance, was unable to hand down their power positions to the next generations in the same way as property is inherited in capitalist countries. This also runs counter to the theory of domination of the new class over the working class.

For me the Soviet Union represents a special type of industrial society. In the Soviet model power resources in production were divided along the same lines as in capitalism. There were managers, experts, supervisors, and workers. However, there were no positions based on the ownership of the means of production, and consequently there was no bourgeoisie or petty bourgeoisie in the country. Class relations did, however, have a very special nature, on account of the links between political power and economy. Overall the social system in the Soviet Union was an extremely slippery object for sociological analysis on account of the power structures of the Communist Party. This was a distinctive feature of the Soviet Union, i.e. the co-existence of the power structure of the Communist Party and the industrial-organizational structures.

The Class Structure of Contemporary Russian Society

The Soviet Union was always a worker society. In line with the Marxist tradition the communist ideology stressed the role of the industrial working class as a leading force in society. In reality, however, agricultural workers and unskilled manual labourers represented the biggest social groups until the 1960s. Since then skilled workers have emerged as a major social category.

The intelligentsia and managerial groups remained comparatively small groups until World War II, but since then began to grow very rapidly. In the late 1970s managerial groups accounted for about one-quarter of the economically active population.

Table 1
Soviet social structure in 1939 and 1979 (%)

	1939	1979
Unskilled manual workers	64	29
Skilled manual workers	19	41
Unskilled white-collar workers	8	5
Skilled white-collar workers	9	25
Total	100	100

Source: Gordon and Nazimova 1986, 13.

Before the collapse of the Soviet system at the beginning of the 1990s, the working class accounted for just over half of the employed population. Within the working class, skilled and unskilled groups were roughly of the same size. Another dividing line within the working class runs between 'white-collar' and 'blue-collar' positions. According to Nikula (1997, 85), about one-third of the Soviet working class were in white-collar positions at the beginning of the 1990s. This implies that the service sector accounted for about one-third of the whole working class, while the remaining two-thirds were employed in manufacturing industries.

New social divisions based on ownership have been emerging in Russia since the collapse of the state socialist system. However, entrepreneurs still account for no more than some five per cent of the economically active population. Power relations in production are also in a state of flux: managers have taken on an increasingly important role in the workplace, at the same time as workers have seen their powers decline.

One of the most prominent analysts of Russian society, Tatiana Zaslavskaya says in a recent description of the current social structure that Russian society today consists of four social strata: the upper, middle, basic and lower strata as well as the desocialized social bottom (Zaslavskaya 1997, 10–11).

The top stratum, according to Zaslavskaya, is the real ruling stratum in society, comprising elite and sub-elite groups that control the political and economic power structures. The middle stratum consists of businessmen, managers, bureaucrats and specialists. As yet it remains numerically quite small, but is expected to play a very major role in the modernization of Russia. The basic stratum, then, accounts for more than two-thirds of Russian society. It represents the average in the country, including large parts of the intelligentsia, white-collar workers and blue-collar workers. The lower stratum comprises the victims of social change, consisting of the elderly, people with a low level of education and those with health problems. Finally, the social bottom is completely isolated from mainstream society. It comprises criminals, prostitutes, alcoholics, and so on (ibid., 11–12). In numerical terms the social structure looks like this:

Upper stratum	1%
Middle stratum	24%
Basic stratum	68%
Social bottom	7%

Zaslavskaya's analysis is based on notions of social stratification in which the main determinants of different strata are education and incomes.

In what follows it is my intention to look at Russian society more closely by using the tools of sociological class analysis. I am interested in social relations, and particularly power relations within the sphere of production.

The analysis is based on representative survey data collected in October-November 1998. The data comprise the whole of the Russian Federation and a total of 2500 personal interviews. The fieldwork was done by the Institute of Sociology at the Russian Academy of Sciences (Moscow), with funding provided by the Academy of Finland. A similar data set was collected in 1991 in the European parts of the Russian federation (N=2149). The data from the two surveys are directly comparable, providing a unique opportunity to monitor the social changes that have happened in Russian society during the 1990s.

In theoretical terms the analysis is grounded in the work of Erik Olin Wright (see e.g. 1978, 1997) as well as myself (Melin 1996). In my earlier papers I have presented a more detailed analysis of the Soviet class structure (ibid.). The class typology I use in this paper is based on Wright's most recent theory (Wright 1997).

Wright's principal tool in the building of his class theory is the concept of exploitation, which is operationalized into three dimensions, i.e. ownership, authority and skills. Empirically, these dimensions are defined by position in the division of labour, authority relations/positions and occupations.

Wright's class typology			
Capitalists	Expert managers	Skilled managers	Non-skilled managers
Small employers	Expert supervisors	Skilled supervisors	Non-skilled supervisors
Petty bourgeoisie	Experts	Skilled workers	Non-skilled workers

Before we proceed to look at the Russian class structure within the employed population, it is useful to examine the overall social structure in Russia in the 1990s. Table 2 presents figures for the whole population aged 18–65. In the early 1990s the Soviet Union was a labour society in transition. Over two-thirds of the population were in gainful employment. The number of pensioners was low, even though retirement age was also low. This was due to the fact that large numbers of pensioners were still working. Unemployment was not recognized in state socialism, and the official figures for people out of work were around one per cent. The number of housewives was also smaller than in Western countries, on the other hand the number of students was comparatively high.

Table 2
Russian social structure in 1991 and 1998 (%)

	1991	1998
Currently employed	71	54
Pensioners	19	28
Unemployed	1	10
Housewives	4	5
Students	7	3
Total	100	100
N	2157	2467

Labour market participation today remains at a relatively high level, with over half of the adult population in gainful employment. Just over one-quarter of the population is retired. Retirement age in Russia is lower than it is in the EU. The official unemployment figures are still very low at around ten per cent, and our survey findings confirm that the numbers out of work are lower than in the EU on average. In the Soviet system women played a very important role in the labour force, and the number of housewives was extremely small. In this respect there has been very little change over the past ten years: only some five per cent of the respondents were classified as housewives. Students account for three per cent of the population, considerably less than at the beginning of the decade.

The biggest change in the social structure has followed from the growth of unemployment and the decline in active employment. Unemployment today is ten times higher than at the beginning of the 1990s, and the share of the working population has declined by more than 30 per cent. Table 3 describes the Russian class structure in 1991 and 1998 using Wright's typology. The main picture that emerges from this analysis is that Russia is still very much a working class society, as it was during the Soviet era, but the nature of society has nonetheless changed.

Table 3
Russian class structure in 1991 and 1998 (%)*

	1991	1998
Managers	15	11
Supervisors	12	9
Experts	15	10
Unskilled workers	28	39
Skilled workers	30	31
Total	100	100
N	1460	1244

* The figures in this Table are based on calculations comprising the wage labour population. In 1991 there were no entrepreneurs at all, in 1998 they accounted for about three per cent of the economically active population.

In 1991 experts with a university degree accounted for 15 per cent of the economically active population (experts are here defined exclusively on the basis of education, without giving any consideration to the nature of their job). In the early 1970s, official statistics indicated that the intelligentsia accounted for roughly the same proportion, but that figure also comprised part of the managers.

Ten years ago one-quarter of the gainfully employed population occupied managerial positions. Some 15 per cent were in top managerial positions, the rest were in supervisory and other lower-level positions. A comparison of the former Soviet Union with the Nordic countries shows that the number of managerial positions in state socialism actually exceeded the corresponding number in advanced capitalist countries. All managerial groups were in fact larger in the Soviet Union than in the Nordic countries.

What exactly has changed in Russia? How have the ongoing structural changes impacted the class structure? The most visible new element in the Russian class structure is clearly the emergence of entrepreneurs. In the absence of reliable registers it is virtually impossible to produce any exact figures on the size of the Russian bourgeoisie and petty bourgeoisie, but our results indicate that entrepreneurial groups account for some three per cent of the economically active population. The true number of entrepreneurs is quite apparently bigger than this, though there does remain the question of whether running a stall at a flea market or driving a taxi as a second job qualifies as entrepreneurship.

Secondly, the number of managers and managerial positions has clearly declined in Russia since the beginning of the 1990s. On the other hand, the number of lower supervisory positions has not decreased to the same extent since the collapse of state socialism. These changes can be explained by reference to the new relations of production. The old double structures (political and economic) of decision-making and power have been replaced by more efficient arrangements that are adequate to the capitalist mode of production. This, in turn, has implied a concentration of power in work organizations. In today's Russia some 10 per cent of the working population are different kinds of experts. The share of experts has shown some decline since the beginning of the 1990s. This is explained by the collapse of the Communist Party structures as well as economic and social planning structures.

A third important result that emerges from our analysis is that the Russian working class has actually grown since the collapse of state socialism. In particular, the share of unskilled workers has increased. This is explained by changes in the use of labour power. Today, for financial reasons, the preference in business companies is for unskilled positions instead of skilled positions. In practice what this means is that Russia has been proletarianized: the working class now accounts for some 70 per cent of the economically active population. When the sharp increase in unemployment is additionally taken into account, it is clear that the changes have meant social decline for quite large groups in Russian society.

These results are at sharp variance with some other recent interpretations of Russian society. Markku Kivinen (1999), for instance, argues that Russia has transformed into a middle class society. According to Kivinen the middle classes represent almost 70 per cent of the population, the working class no more than one-third. These results are based on a survey conducted in St.Petersburg in 1996. However, it is clear that the theoretical approach adopted by Kivinen very much overestimates the impact of certain structural changes. He puts too much weight on the labour process and fails to attach enough importance to other relations of power and dominance.

The picture I have drawn suggests that the middle class accounts for one-third of the population and the working class for the remaining 70 per cent. Managerial groups represent just over one-fifth, experts about 10 per cent of the Russian class structures. These results are more or less in line with self-reports according to which over 75 per cent say they do not occupy managerial or supervisory positions. Only two per cent identified themselves with top management, 13 per cent with middle management and nine per cent with lower management.

The picture is somewhat different if we also take account of the factor of gender. Women in the former Soviet Union were better placed than women in most Western countries to get an education for themselves and to pursue a career. This has very much changed during the 1990s: by now male and female positions in Russia are characterized by a certain gender specificity. Men occupy managerial positions more often than women, who in turn are in expert positions more often than men.

Two-thirds of all entrepreneurs are men. The only group in which there are the same number of women as men is that of supervisors. Women predominate most clearly in the group of experts, of whom 80 per cent are women. Women occupy expert positions four times as often as men.

In advanced capitalist countries the working class has been female-dominated for decades. In Finland, for instance, women account for roughly two-thirds of the working class. The picture in Russia is very different, with women representing half of the working class. The situation is the same among skilled and unskilled workers. On the other hand, men belong to the working class more often than women: among men some 75 per cent are currently in the working class, while the figure for women is 66 per cent.

So what has happened during the past decade? Since the beginning of the 1990s the proportion of female managers has shown some tendency to increase. This is largely explained by the growth of new, expanded labour markets. In particular, the service sector offers new positions for female managerial staff (shops, restaurants, consultancies, etc.). In Russia there are still more female than male experts, although the number of men in expert positions has increased during the past decade and the number of women has come down.

Table 4
Russian class structure by gender in 1998 (%)

	Men	Women	Total
Entrepreneurs	4	2	3
Managers	10	10	10
Supervisors	7	9	9
Experts	4	15	10
Skilled workers	32	29	30
Unskilled workers	42	35	38
Total	100	100	100
N	587	657	1244

The process of proletarianization has been more outstanding among men than among women. In particular, the unskilled male labour force has shown strong growth since the beginning of the 1990s. This is due in part to changes in the Russian labour markets, which with the process of privatization has seen a movement towards Taylorization.

Class Situation

In our earlier studies we have introduced a research strategy for class analysis which we call the 'scope logic approach to class analysis' (Blom et al. 1992). The strategy is based on the notion that there are different levels, or stages, in class analysis. We need to start out with an analysis of class structure and then move on to the structuration of class situation. A synthesis of these levels will then take us to an analysis of consciousness and organization. Finally, following a synthesis of the previous levels, we can proceed to the relationship between classes and the formation of social forces (ibid., 31-35).

In the discussion above I have provided a detailed description of the Russian class structure. I will now move on to analyse the structuration of class situation by looking at incomes, education, authority relations, decision-making and subjective evaluations of general well-being.

Incomes

As we have seen the results of our survey suggest that there has been a general tendency of proletarianization in Russia. To what extent can this tendency be substantiated; to what extent is it simply a product of our imagination? One indicator of social differentiation is provided by incomes. For Table 5 below I have calculated a simple income index for different class groups: the average monthly income is 100.

It is immediately clear from these figures that income differentials have increased in Russia. During the state socialist period the distribution of incomes was relatively even, but by the early 1990s the differences were already beginning to grow. Today, the wage gap between managers and workers is quite considerable – and in fact comes quite close to the respective Finnish figure.

Table 5
Classes and incomes in 1991 and 1998 (mean=100)

	Women		Men		Total	
	1991	1998	1991	1998	1991	1998
Expert managers	115	133	152	239	139	185
Skilled managers	97	100	160	104	136	104
Expert supervisors	106	140	120	179	113	156
Skilled supervisors	102	88	130	146	119	114
Experts	87	90	117	181	96	108
Skilled workers	72	69	112	101	92	85
Non-skilled workers	67	61	106	102	83	82

The most dramatic changes in incomes have happened not between male and female employees, but within the genders. Wage differentials have increased most among women. Having said that it is important to stress that there are also huge differences between the earnings of men and women. Even during state socialism men earned more than women, but the gap was not nearly as big as it is in capitalist countries. At the beginning of the 1990s male managers earned twice as much as non-skilled women, by now this difference has increased four times over.

There are, on the other hand, some groups in which the wage differentials have actually decreased. One example is provided by the group of skilled managers, where women have managed to reduce the wage gap. There is a similar situation among skilled workers. Overall, however, the trend towards greater inequality can be expected to continue in the new millennium. In particular, we may expect to see a continued increase in the salaries of managers and experts (professionals). The working class, on the other hand, does not have the resources to fight for better wages.

Education

The Soviet system designed and created massive educational institutions, offering people good opportunities for vocational and higher education. One of the distinctive features of this system was its high degree of specialization: it produced large numbers of specialists with a very narrow area of expertise rather than a general intelligentsia. A new feature of the 1990s has been the launch of private institutions in the field of higher education: there are now hundreds of private universities and polytechnics throughout the country. The introduction of tuition fees is another new feature. Taken together, these changes mean there is now increased elitism in Russian higher education.

Table 6
Highest level of education by class in 1991 and 1998 (%)*

	1991		1998	
	Tech	Univ	Tech	Univ
Expert managers	20	76	23	73
Skilled managers	26	64	21	52
Expert supervisors	10	87	30	64
Skilled supervisors	37	44	31	40
Experts	25	68	34	55
Skilled workers	25	26	18	29
Non-skilled workers	19	8	17	9

* TECH = Technicum, college, UNIV = University degree.

The legacy of the former Soviet system is clearly seen in our results, i.e. the overall level of education in Russia is still high. Almost all expert managers have at least a college degree, and the same goes for expert supervisors and experts. Over one-quarter of skilled workers have a university degree, almost one-fifth of non-skilled workers have a college degree. But how can a non-skilled worker have a university degree in the first place? In Wright's typology non-skilled labourer does not refer to the individual and his or her qualifications, but is defined as a position in the division of labour. In other words, a sociologist who works as a cab driver is classified as a non-skilled worker.

It is quite clear from these results that the Russian economy is wasting its human resources: large numbers of people are in jobs for which they have far too high qualifications. On the other hand the educational level of managerial groups has shown a tendency to decline.

Authority and Decision-Making

In the Soviet Union the means of production were owned by the state, the Communist Party was involved in economic decision-making, and industrial production was based on national planning. All these features meant that there were several levels as well as parallel managerial structures; which in turn meant that there were more managerial positions in the Soviet Union than in capitalist countries.

The communist ideology was that workers were masters in their own house, and indeed in state socialist countries workers enjoyed more autonomy than their colleagues in capitalist countries. Our comparison between Finland and Soviet Estonia in the 1980s showed that in Estonia, one in three industrial workers had supervisory responsibilities while the corresponding figure for Finland was one in ten. In Estonia the job required mental effort or decision-making more often than in Finland (Blom et al. 1991, 352).

The Russian work organization has seen many changes during the 1990s, but there has also been a certain element of continuity. The main trend is that managers have seen an increase in their power resources, workers by contrast have seen their power resources dwindle. This means that there are fewer positions of authority than there were earlier. According to our results one-fifth or 21 per cent have supervisory responsibilities, which is less than during the socialist era. These changes imply that Russian businesses are now adopting capitalist ways of organizing work.

Our empirical findings confirm the emergence of new managerial practices. Today there are fewer managers, supervisors and workers with supervisory duties and responsibilities than there were ten years ago. It seems that managers have gained more supervisory authority, while the powers of supervisors have decreased to some extent. Our survey results suggest that there have been no changes in this respect in the situation of workers.

Table 7
Supervisory positions and supervisory duties in 1998 (% yes)*

	1998
Expert managers	89
Skilled managers	89
Expert supervisors	72
Skilled supervisors	87
Experts	1
Skilled workers	2
Non-skilled workers	–
Total	17

* Direct comparisons between the two surveys are not possible because of slight differences in the wording of the question concerning supervisory duties.

In the Soviet Union managers had very little say in decisions concerning products or the volume of production. On the other hand, they did exercise control over the actual production process, i.e. they could make decisions concerning work organization, methods, number of employees, etc. In this respect they were indeed real masters in their own house.

As for decision-making at plant level, industrial workers once again had more power in the Soviet Union than colleagues in Western countries. In principle the managerial system was based on 'one-man management', but because of a constant lack of labour workers had important power resources at the shopfloor level. Since the collapse of state socialism Russian enterprises have started to adopt Western managerial practices. Our results show that with the advance of privatization, managerial power has increased at the same time as workers have seen their former resources dwindle.

During the past decade there have been deep-going changes in terms of participation in decision-making. The old planning and party organs no longer have the power to control and direct factory managers. At the same time owners have assumed an increasingly important role in decision-making. The changes in managerial power have followed a somewhat contradictory path. Our baseline hypothesis was that managers' power resources have increased as a result of privatization. In some respects it seems that this has indeed been the case, but there are certain areas in which managers today have less power than they did during the last years of perestroika.

Managers today have much less say in hiring and sacking workers than they did ten years ago. How can this difference be explained? To me the logical interpretation has to be that financial prudence is far more important today than it was ten years ago, and therefore these decisions are now made by owners. On other dimensions the changes are somewhat less dramatic. Perhaps the most interesting observation is that there has been no increase in managerial power.

Table 8
Participation in decision-making in 1991 and 1998 (% yes)

	Hire & sack		Work load		Budget	
	1991	1998	1991	1998	1991	1998
Expert managers	60	24	78	76	49	46
Skilled managers	65	40	74	87	35	27
Expert supervisors	–	–	–	–	–	–
Skilled supervisors	–	–	–	–	–	–
Experts	5	–	9	5	9	3
Skilled workers	2	1	6	5	3	1
Non-skilled workers	1	–	3	3	1	–

Our results run counter to the assumption that managerial power has increased with privatization and the emergence of Russian capitalism. Managers play a significant role at plant level, and they possess significant supervisory powers. They are also decision-makers, but their power resources have not increased during the past decade.

Changes in Well-Being

There was no unemployment in the Soviet Union; in fact there was a constant shortage of labour. During the past decade unemployment has started to increase, rising from an initially very low level to the current figure of 10 per cent. People out of work represented the second biggest category in the economically active population, accounting for 20 per cent. The biggest group was that of pensioners, who accounted for 52 per cent of the non-active population.

In Russia today unemployment is very clearly a class matter. Unemployment is much more common in the working class than it is among managerial groups, where the problem is virtually non-existent. The main group affected is that of non-skilled labour.

Part-time employment was also a comparatively rare phenomenon in the Soviet Union, as the dominant labour market ideology favoured full-time jobs. In some EU countries more than one-fifth of the labour force currently work on a part-time basis, whereas in Russia the corresponding figure is 14 per cent. Although this is clearly below the EU average, it is nonetheless somewhat higher than the figures in Finland, for instance.

Many observers have noted that the majority of the Russian population have experienced social decline during the past decade. In particular, large numbers have seen their financial situation deteriorate, at the same time as a small elite have been making small fortunes. Over 80 per cent of the respondents said their material well-being had declined since 1988, while only six per cent reported an improvement. The question of well-being also ties in closely with class position.

In 1991, the respondents in our survey were asked how they expected the financial situation of their family to develop over the next five years, with three preset options: decline, remain unchanged, and improve. In the 1998 survey, the respondents were asked how their financial situation had changed since 1988, with the preset options ranging from much better to much worse.

Our results indicate that in 1991, the general climate in Russia was characterized by a strong sense of optimism. The working class in particular was looking ahead to a brighter future. Workers expected to see an improvement in the financial situation more often than other social groups. Managerial groups did not expect to see any major changes. The most striking result is that non-skilled workers were the most optimistic group, while managerial groups had more modest hopes about the future.

Table 9
Changes in well-being between 1991 and 1998 (%)

	1991	1998	1998
	Will improve	Has improved	Has worsened
Expert managers	5	12	80
Skilled managers	11	18	78
Expert supervisors	5	10	77
Skilled supervisors	4	2	90
Experts	13	7	85
Skilled workers	27	6	86
Non-skilled workers	31	4	87

How, then, have things actually turned out? We have all read about the constant crisis of the Russian economy and its dwindling performance. A heavy devaluation of the Russian rouble in autumn 1998 brought a dramatic reduction in the purchasing power of households. The effects of these developments are clearly reflected in our results. In 1998 only four per cent of non-skilled workers said their financial situation has improved during the past 10 years, almost 90 per cent said it had deteriorated. A greater proportion of managers than workers indicated their financial situation had improved. There were clear differences between individual groups, but even so only less than one-fifth of skilled managers (who were the most optimistic group) indicated positive changes. In 1998 skilled supervisors were most pessimistic about their financial situation.

Conclusions

During the past 15 years there has been intense and sometimes heated debate about the relevance of class research and class theory. Some sociologists have taken the position that the concept of class is inadequate for purposes of explaining social divisions in post-modern society (see e.g. Pakulski 1993). The death-of-classes argument is justified by reference to changes in voting behaviour (decline in class voting), changes in trade union organizations (decline in union affiliation) and changes in work organization (less conflicts). On the other hand, some researchers have launched major research programmes in an attempt to analyse classes in contemporary capitalism (see e.g. Wright 1997).

Russia can by no means be described as a typical European market society. In certain respects Russia is at the very beginning of the path of capitalist development, with the process of original accumulation still under way. The national wealth that was accumulated during the state socialist era is currently being redistributed via privatization. The markets in Russia as well as market behaviour (in the Weberian sense) are also still developing. As a result of all these changes there have emerged new social divisions. Russia is an extremely interesting case from the point of view of class analysis and presents a good test case for the relevance of class analysis.

In state socialism the class structure was determined by political and economic factors. In contemporary Russia, there are divisions that are based more and more on power and ownership relations in production. The position of almost all social groups is determined by whether or not they own the means of production and by the kind of organizational power assets they possess in the workplace.

Russia today is a class society where social differentiation has increased very dramatically during the past ten years or so. We have witnessed the birth of a new elite, that of 'new Russians' (cf. Bäckman 1998). During the early 1990s the old economic and political elite, or the nomenklatura, had *de facto* control and to an extent also had partial ownership of major economic assets. This old elite also constitutes the hard core of the new Russians. It has been estimated that the new elite accounts for around one per cent of the population: these are the people who have emerged as the true winners of the ongoing process of transformation.

Another group who have certainly benefited is represented by managers, who have gained considerably in economic power with privatization. At the same time they have managed to hold on to their key position as an integral part of local and regional power elites.

The vast majority of the Russian population have seen economic and social decline: over three-quarters of our respondents said their financial situation had deteriorated during the past ten years. Only less than one per cent indicated they had no problems with money. According to our results the biggest social class in Russia is represented by the working class, while unskilled workers are the biggest single social category. This also implies that old qualifications are quite simply no longer enough today.

Unemployment is a growing and serious problem for Russia. Large numbers of people have also had trouble getting their employers to pay their wages, and social benefits have decreased. This, combined with the devaluation of the Russian rouble in 1998, has meant that Russian society has been proletarianized. Indeed one utopia has now come true: the majority of the population belongs to the proletariat.

The future of Russia:

- a small and unstable elite with ample power resources
- a relatively small middle class with limited power resources
- a large working class with limited power resources
- a growing underclass

What, then, does the future hold for Russia? My sociological guess is that the middle class in Russia will remain relatively small and economically and politically weak for quite some while to come. The working class will remain the biggest social class in the country, though it will certainly not become a 'class for itself'. The ruling elite will remain small, but there will be severe contests between different elite fractions.

Chapter 2

Social Mobility in Russian Society

Michail Chernish

Origins of Mobility Patterns in Soviet Society

High social mobility has been regarded by Russian citizens as a major achievement of Russian, formerly Soviet society in the twentieth century. Soon after the seizure of power in 1917, the Bolsheviks set out to provide new opportunities for the formerly 'oppressed' classes – poor peasants and workers. Wider opportunities for the offspring of peasants and workers arose mainly from deliberate policies and unintended outcomes of revolutionary change and civil war. State bureaucracy positions were vacated en masse by persecuted functionaries of the old Tsarist state apparatus. Soon after the revolution and in the course of the civil war, over three million 'enemy elements' including top Tsarist bureaucrats left the country. Close to 1.5 million such elements, including former army officers, were killed in the Civil war fighting. The leading positions were quickly filled by 'friendly' elements including revolutionary intelligentsia or workers capable of guiding new institutions of the revolutionary state. In the same breath, the authorities issued new laws limiting the rights for mobility for strata regarded as inimical towards the revolution and Soviet power. On January 21, 1924, the Second Congress of Soviets adopted a new Constitution of the Soviet State that banned a number of categories of the population from 'taking part in the running of the Soviet State'. The groups in question were kulaks (rich peasants) and their children, priests and their offspring, former policemen, traders and their family members. It is not known precisely how many Soviet citizens were affected by the ban, but the Soviet historian G. Eskov estimated the number so maltreated at 3.5 per cent of rural and 7.7 per cent of urban dwellers, or 6.7 million Soviet citizens (Eskov 1983). The Constitution did not specifically limit the opportunities of social mobility for the mentioned categories. But, as Vladimir Ilyin rightly points out, the stripping of civil rights from a citizen was a stigma that was conducive to harsher consequences including a ban on entry into educational institutions of higher learning or occupancy of any positions of social importance (Gosudarstvo, 1996).

The policy of repression levelled at the elements of the old regime came hand in hand with a policy of social favouritism accorded to friendly social classes such as workers or poor peasants. The leader of the Soviet regime Vladimir Lenin vowed to teach 'a kitchen maid to run a state'. In 1919 the Bolshevik regime set up new educational institutions (*rabfak*) providing crash courses of higher learning for the offspring of workers and peasants. The role of *rabfaks* grew significantly after the Communist Party proclaimed a course of rapid industrialization. From 1928 to 1940 the number of students in the Soviet Union increased five times over, reaching the figure of 812,000. The census of 1937 showed that the non-manual labour force numbered 13 million. From 1925 to 1940, the number of workers and office workers increased from 2.5 million to 36 million (SSSR, 1977, p. 145).

Social mobility increased significantly as a result of the collectivization policy, which boosted the number of managerial positions in rural areas by 580,000 (ibid., p. 149). These positions were occupied by 'socially friendly elements', i.e. poor peasants or workers.

The scale of upward mobility for formerly underprivileged groups was further increased by the expansion of the Red Army. In 1925 the new Law on universal military duty was adopted. The Law provided for the creation of a wide network of military schools and academies whose main objective was to train a new corps of professional military officers to replace the 'military specialists' coming from the old Tsarist army. By 1939 the Red Army maintained 14 military academies and 63 infantry army schools, 14 navy schools and 32 air force schools. The officer corps of the Red Army kept rising until 1941 when it stood at about 500,000 men (ibid., p. 181).

The opportunities for upward mobility came to be linked with the mounting pressure of the Great Terror. There are varying estimates as to how many top positions were vacated by the Stalinist purges. The British historian R. Conquest assessed the number of Soviet citizens purged at nine million. Official Russian estimates are more modest: 2.5 million. Whatever the assessment, it is obvious that apart from other objectives the Terror solved an important problem of rotating personnel at top managerial positions, providing new chances for mobility for young Soviet careerists.

Mobility as a Cultural Ideal

Equality and chances of upward mobility came to be one of the most prominent ideals of Soviet society. The most symbolic of Soviet songs that came close to becoming recognized as an official anthem of the Soviet Union proclaimed that there was no other country in the world apart from the USSR 'where a man could breathe so freely'; this was the only land where 'there is a road for the young and honour for the old everywhere'. Alongside other important themes (mythology of the revolution, Russian history), the mobility idea became an emphatic line in popular Soviet movies. In key movies of the period it became the most important message passed on by the Soviet state to its citizens. The first Soviet sound movie was called 'The trip ticket to the future', telling the tale of homeless children and hardened criminals who were reformed by the process of socialist construction and who rose above their past to become shock workers sharing the goals of service to the state. In a way the message of the film was a substitute for the salvation theme so common in a country that had recently been Christian. The 'Head train' film spoke about a similar quasi-religious transformation of industrial workers who embraced the socialist way of thinking and came to contemplate new horizons of upward mobility. The specific feature of the communist propaganda, as observed by Hannah Arendt (1968, 43), consisted in threats of 'missing the train of history, with remaining hopelessly behind their time, with spending their lives uselessly'. The rewards of moving with the times provided by the regime emerged as new life chances and in particular with the chances of achieving a new position of respect and power in a society where power was a key resource. In no other film was this statement so obvious as in 'The way of light' (1940, directed by G. Alexandrov), where an ordinary woman worker ends up in Moscow as a member of Soviet nobility in possession of the vast resources of the Soviet state. She achieves ultimate happiness and is portrayed as riding a lacquered limousine amid clouds singing a song glorifying the 'way of light' opened up for her by the Soviet regime. The 'Member of the government' film tells a similar tale of striking achievement by an ordinary Russian woman who through her dedicated toils and ultimate support of Bolshevik ideals rises from an inferior position to become a member of top Soviet leadership.

In the 1930s and 1940s the Soviet propaganda emphasized the following dimensions of mobility open to Soviet citizens:

Mobility of status. The major statement of Soviet propaganda stressed that by hard work and loyalty to the communist ideals, the ordinary citizen could achieve a higher status of acceptance from the authorities and become a) a shock worker, b) a respected citizen, c) a martyr whose name would be etched in the regime's tables of honour. It is notable that status mobility opportunities were usually accorded to socially inferior elements such as peasants, women, criminals, or former white guard officers. In the mythology of the regime a worker was a high enough status and his 'way of light' could only direct him towards the groups of 'stakhanovites' embodying the best qualities of the socialist working class.

Mobility of power. The statement passed on by the communist authorities to its citizens stated plainly that any 'kitchenmaid' could become a member of the government and any dumb-witted peasant could rise to a position of kolkhoz chairman if only they showed themselves to be capable of assuming responsibility for the fulfilment of the plans and vehemently opposed the schemes of backward elements (socially retarded peasants, bourgeois specialists, hidden enemies). Though attaining a sublime position of power, the arriving elements could never hope to become ultimate leaders of the Soviet state, a position reserved for the old revolutionaries who posed as unwavering keepers of the ideals.

Territorial mobility. A loyal and hard working Soviet citizen could hope at some point of his life to move from his town or village to the city of Moscow. The capital of the Soviet Union was glorified in films and books as a special utopia of striking beauty where any dreams could be fulfilled. This statement was most prominent in the 'Pig breeder and cattleman', a key movie (1941) that portrayed a young woman of humble peasant origins who through her hard work achieved the status of a stakhanovite, won the right to show her achievements at the National Exhibition in Moscow and met there the man of her life, a Georgian cattleman. In the film Moscow was represented as a universal melting pot that did away with cultural differences and emphasized other, socialist criteria of social distinction. In the cultural space delineated by communist propaganda, social mobility was also firmly linked with the exploration of new remote areas. The 'Komsomolsk' film (1938, directed by A. Gerasimov) portrayed socialist construction in remote Far Eastern regions where young communist youth found ample opportunity to assert themselves and win a new status. The reality was a striking contrast to that portrayed in the film: camp inmates rather than young communists were a key element of the labour force used in the city's construction.

Mobility to better living standards. Communist propaganda never portrayed material achievements as a major objective of human enterprise. Better living standards came naturally to those who willingly participated in socialist construction or won special distinction in fighting the regime's enemies. It was assumed that wealth, if it became life's major purpose, could have a corrupting influence on an individual, swaying him or her from the path of honour and true achievement to the road of degeneration.

The sustenance of high mobility rates in the early days of the communist regime served several purposes. Firstly, upward mobility appeared as a substitute of social legitimization for the regime based on the widespread use of terror and total control over all spheres of public life. By taking advantage of the new opportunities for social advancement offered by the regime, Soviet citizens directly or indirectly shared the responsibility for the repressive strategies employed to heighten mobility rates. Secondly, in the absence of free popular ballot, high social mobility served as a means to reduce the symbolic distance between the rulers and the ruled. Thirdly, high social mobility served as proof of the unchanging objective of communist power to modernize Russian society by providing education and opportunities for social advancement to the majority of its citizens.

The Soviet dream was in many respects similar to the American one. It is not accidental that the Soviet-made film 'Moscow does not believe in tears' that portrayed a humble Russian girl who braved life's problems to become the top manager of a big textile plant, won an Oscar in the USA in 1982. Both cultural codes stressed hard toil and consistency of action as the main road to success. Both dreams underlined the role of education as a channel of mobility. There were, however, a few significant cultural differences between them. Unlike the American dream, the Soviet one always emphasized the unbreakable link between individual achievement and service to the state. A cowboy who amassed wealth by herding cattle through dangerous areas would never be a great hero in the Soviet Union. From the Soviet point of view a major fault of his achievement was that he served himself instead of working for the public good. The Soviet dream could only become reality if a Soviet citizen shared the main tenets of communist ideology. In other words, the Soviet dream came to be realized through political conformism and a predestined line of action rather than independence and individualism. A new status was never won by the Soviet citizen alone, it was bestowed upon him by the authorities that posed as ultimate referees of all human achievement.

Some of the attitudes to success came to mellow in the later years of the regime. The gradual embourgeoisement of Soviet lifestyles and a stronger emphasis on better living standards whetted public appetites for better quality goods. The growing individualism of urban society created preconditions for the acceptance of variance in wealth that had hitherto been qualified as alien to Soviet society. However, key attitudes to social mobility remained unchanged. Equality of opportunity has always been a paramount condition of Russian life. Individual achievement can only be called true success if it contributes to the public good and strengthens the power of the Russian state. The stereotypes mentioned largely explain the prevailing attitudes to the 'new Russians', the nouveaux-riches of Russia. They are detested and ridiculed by the population because their rise to wealth is viewed as illegitimate and self-serving. The same critical stance is reserved for bankers and traders. The fact that they do not always contribute to increased production suffices to brand them as useless spongers making money out of air.

Generational Life Course

The classical theory of mobility stressed the universal character of mobility patterns. Changes in the economy and political transformation came to be regarded as the main factor of social advancement or failure. The long-term mobility patterns that Lipset and Bendix (1967) observed in Western societies resulted from a) economic change (changes in demand for performance), and b) changes in the supply of talent (the degree of democratization of the educational system and political change). The latter was qualified as having concomitant rather than decisive effects. There may be more mobility in one country than in another, Lipset and Bendix (1967, 67) say, and yet less opportunity. 'For example, if a country is 90 per cent peasant, even with completely equal opportunity most children of peasants must remain peasants.' However, the example of the Soviet Union clearly indicates that this pattern can be broken. Even with 90 per cent peasants, a country like the Soviet Union succeeded in bringing its mobility to a fairly high level. In other words, while the scale and the pattern of mobility may be similar, the basic factors of mobility may be different and in many cases non-economic factors can have a greater impact than economic ones. This fact was highlighted by Goldthorpe in his key book 'The constant flux'. Goldthorpe stresses that the mobility pattern is a pretty stable social phenomenon, at least in Europe where little change in mobility displacement could have occurred despite the numerous cataclysms of European history. According to Goldthorpe two European nations – Britain and France – underpin the European pattern of mobility or 'the core mobility' that can be instrumental in describing social flux in most other European nations. Goldthorpe makes no consistent effort to further explore his striking discovery. What is the essence of the 'core mobility'? What reality stands behind the concept? Why is it so stable and why is it so universal, at least in Europe? Is it a specific European pattern of mobility, historically and culturally defined and immutable throughout that turbulent history of the European continent? Why do exceptions occur, such as in Ireland? Can the 'core mobility' concept be applicable to other parts of the world, to China, for instance, and on what conditions? The opposing view claims that mobility is always determined by a cluster of specific circumstances and is shaped by the country's history, politics and patterns of daily behaviour. Goldthorpe qualifies this approach to mobility as 'exceptionalist'. The 'exceptionalists' deny any possible common core to mobility in different countries and regard the process as a unique one. Summing up, we can say that there are three possible points of view from which mobility can be studied. It can be regarded as a pattern of social flux characterizing a certain stage of development. Sorokin (1992) was the first to formulate the key elements of the concept. The Western society treading the path of industrial development and political openness gradually reaches a stage of development when a) the social barriers to mobility are collapsing, b) upward mobility decreases the number of peasants to the point where the urban population prevails over the rural one, and c) the middle class becomes a significant stratum and the main agent of political life. The concept came to be slightly modified in the mobility theory of Lipset and Bendix, but its main components remained intact: the closer a society is to the industrial stage, the more mobility it is bound to have. This romantic 'universalist' view of mobility came to be questioned by Goldthorpe and earlier by D. Featherman (1982). For them, there is an obvious 'western' or European pattern of mobility that comes through when only the 'net' outcome is counted. The marginal 'exceptionalist' theory, as was stated above, denies any facts that bespeak of 'cores' or universalist mobility pattern.

Our own exploration of Russian history allows to us speculate that the 'core mobility' concept can have little heuristic power in Russian conditions. It can be speculated that the similarity of European mobility is born out of a characteristic relationship between politics and economy that emerged on the continent a long time ago. Economic development, though related to political action, remains relatively independent and is guided by its own specific set of values. Not so in Russia, where the relationship between economy and politics has always been much closer, culminating in a state-run economy in the Soviet era. The state and its political actions have determined the main directions of Russian economic expansion from the very beginning of the Russian state. Economic structures and related political structures in Russia have accordingly been shaped and reshaped far more frequently than the relevant structures in Europe. In our view, a concept that can provide more understanding of Russian mobility patterns is that of a generation. Each generation of Russian history had to meet a specific constellation of circumstances guiding social and economic advancement. We have already mentioned the specific factors that shaped the pattern of mobility characteristic of Soviet society at the incipient stage of its history: industrialization, collectivization, purges and totalitarian mobilization. The pattern provided ample opportunities for upward mobility, generated fear, conformism and high hopes. The post-war period brought about a change of mobility factors. Below are the data that reveal new patterns of mobility. We have divided all Russian citizens into three generations. The first of these is a post-war generation consisting of citizens born before 1950. In most cases, these are Russian citizens aged 55 or older. Given the low life expectancy in contemporary Russia, there are few Russian citizens older than 65. The historic background of that generation is full of dramatic about-turns: post-war reconstruction, the death of Stalin and the end of widespread terror, new plans for the construction of communist society, the Khruschev thaw and attempts at economic reform.

The second generation, now aged from 40 to 55, reached maturity in the late 1960s and 1970s – a period often described in Russia as the 'stagnation era'. Unlike the previous generation, it saw few major events and enjoyed stability until 1985 when Mikhail Gorbachev launched a new reconstruction policy. The third generation consists of Russian citizens aged from 25 to 40. Those born in the 1960s and 1970s had to come to terms with a pretty dramatic change in their lives in the mid-1980s and 1990s: perestroika and glasnost, the collapse of the Soviet Union, a perpetual economic crisis and a fledgling market economy, often crude and deformed. It has become commonplace in Russian sociology to describe the ever-increasing gap between the rich and the poor in the recent Russian history, but it might also be worthwhile to look into possible shifts of social positions caused by ongoing social change.

The Post-War Generation

Table 1
'Post-war generation' position structure (%)

Position	Aged 25	Aged 35	Aged 45	Aged 55
Top manager	0.5	0.6	0.3	0.2
Mid-manager	0.8	1.7	3.2	3.1
Shopfloor manager	3.5	5.9	6.6	4.4
Specialist	11.0	12.8	11.6	6.0
Clerk or technician	26.8	27.5	27.2	16.3
Worker	37.9	38.2	38.3	25.3
Farmer	11.3	9.3	7.4	4.7
Other	8.3	4.0	5.3	40.0
Total	100.0	100.0	100.0	100.0

Table 1 clearly points to the conditions favouring upward mobility. Firstly, the proportion of mid-management positions has increased from less than one per cent to over three per cent by the age of 45. The shopfloor manager group was also growing, providing employment to over six per cent of the population. The group of specialists came to be stable as well as positions of other groups except for that of collective farmers, which was reduced by one-half at the age of 35 and slightly increasing later on.

Table 2
'War generation' mobility: 25–35 years (%)

	Occupation at 35							
	T/M	M/M	S/M	SP	C/T	W	F	Total
Top man	50.0	0.0	0.0	25.0	25.0	0.0	0.0	100.0
Mid-man	0.0	42.9	0.0	0.0	42.9	14.3	0.0	100.0
Shpfl man	0.0	3.4	55.2	6.9	17.2	13.8	0.0	100.0
Spclst	2.2	4.3	4.3	78.5	9.7	1.1	0.0	100.0
Clerk/ techn	0.4	2.2	3.6	5.8	75.6	11.1	1.3	100.0
Worker	0.0	0.0	5.9	1.5	9.3	81.7	1.5	100.0
Farmer	0.0	1.1	0.0	2.1	6.4	20.2	70.2	100.0
Total	0.6	1.8	6.1	12.4	28.9	40.5	9.7	100.0

Table 2 shows the structure of mobility for the 'war generation' between two points of their life course, i.e. 25 and 35 years. The data for top managers cannot be reliable since there are too few of them in the data set. Farmers turned out to be the most mobile group of all. The data show that about one-fifth of those who were farmers at the age of 25 went on to join the group of workers. This tendency is a commonplace phenomenon in all countries that undergo industrialization. Workers had less opportunities of mobility. They mostly rose to occupy positions of shopfloor manager of technician. There were few workers who had a real chance of becoming part of the group of specialists – only 1.5 per cent. The rise to the group of specialists from the group of clerks or technicians appeared to be much easier. In fact almost six per cent of those who started their careers as technicians made their way into the group of specialists.

Specialists experienced mobility in two directions: they rose to become managers of different rank including top managers, but in almost 10 per cent of all cases they dropped into the group of technicians. Specialists almost never went downwards to join the group of workers or farmers.

Shopfloor managers appeared to be less protected. Part of them went up to merge into the group of mid-managers. However, an even larger part of the group fell from their positions to become clerks, technicians, workers or even farmers. The same tendency was seen in mid-managers. There were few of them at the age of 25 and their position was far less stable than that of other age groups.

Table 3
'War generation': social change between 35 and 45 (%)

	Occupation at 45							
	T/M	**M/M**	**S/M**	**SP**	**C/T**	**W**	**F**	**Total**
Top man	20.0	20.0	20.0	20.0	20.0	0.0	0.0	100.0
Mid-man	6.7	60.0	6.7	0.0	20.0	6.7	0.0	100.0
Shpfl man	0.0	15.7	47.1	11.8	13.7	9.8	2.0	100.0
Spclst	0.0	4.7	10.3	72.9	5.6	6.5	0.0	100.0
Clerk/ techn	0.4	0.9	4.4	5.3	80.2	8.4	0.4	100.0
Worker	0.0	0.6	2.5	0.3	7.2	88.7	0.6	100.0
Farmer	0.0	1.3	2.6	0.0	9.0	12.8	74.4	100.0
Total	0.4	3.5	7.1	12.2	28.6	40.5	7.7	100.0

Between ages 25 and 45 the farmer group appeared to be quite active in terms of its mobility. Apart from actively penetrating the group of workers, they also merged with the groups of clerks and technicians. Workers increased their penetration of the group of technicians and also made their way into the group of shopfloor managers. This appeared to be the limit of their careers. There was a minuscule proportion of the working class who made it to the group of specialists. Clerical workers appeared to be more successful in doing so. They actively moved up into the group of specialists and shopfloor managers, but also quite frequently experienced downward mobility towards the group of workers. The group of specialists also experienced social migration in both directions: on the one hand they rose to become shopfloor and mid-managers, on the other hand they slid down to join the group of workers or clerks.

The group of mid-managers had active interaction with the group of clerks and technicians and – to a lesser extent – with the group of top managers.

Table 4
'War generation': social mobility between 45 and 50 (%)

	T/M	M/M	S/M	SP	C/T	W	F	Total
Top man	100.0	0.0	0.0	0.0	0.0	0.0	0.0	100.0
Mid-man	0.0	83.3	0.0	11.1	0.0	0.0	5.6	100.0
Shpfl man	0.0	5.6	63.9	2.8	8.3	16.7	2.8	100.0
Spclst	0.0	6.9	8.6	75.9	6.9	1.7	0.0	100.0
Clerk/ techn	0.7	2.7	3.3	3.3	82.0	6.0	2.0	100.0
Worker	0.0	0.0	2.4	0.0	3.3	91.9	2.4	100.0
Farmer	0.0	2.4	0.0	0.0	2.4	19.5	75.6	100.0
Total	0.4	5.1	7.4	10.1	26.9	42.1	8.0	100.0

Between 45 and 55 there was less upward mobility and, in some cases, obvious decline. About one-fifth of all farmers went on to become workers. This is proof of the tendencies in agriculture: on the one hand, the inflow of machinery turning farmers into agricultural workers, on the other hand the outward mobility of farmers into cities to become low-skilled urban manpower.

By the age of 55 the group of workers found themselves in a situation of little mobility. Only some workers appeared to have changed their social positions. The same is true of clerks and technicians.

At the same time the group of specialists remained mobile, with outlets towards higher social status positions in managerial groups. Shopfloor managers turned out to be the least stable group: by age 55 they began quickly to lose their positions and become workers or clerks. Mid-managers also lost their positions to become specialists or farmers.

The life course of the 'war generation' attests to a fairly mobile situation, with a substantial proportion of the population flowing towards more advanced managerial positions: at an early stage in life to a shopfloor manager status, and later on to a mid-manager position.

The above trends were established by log linear analysis, used to measure the associations between the mentioned points in life.

Table 5
Results of log linear analysis

Two points linked	Partial Chi-square
Occupation at 25 – occupation at 35	183.2
Occupation 35 – occupation 45	106.4
Occupation 45 – occupation 55	283.2

The weakest association was observed between the life course points of 35 and 45 years. This period was the most dynamic one in the life of the 'post war generation'. We calculated the index of mobility equal to the ratio of the number of upward and downward mobility cases in that period. The index figure was 1.65. This means that a large proportion of Russian citizens succeeded in carving out managerial careers for themselves in the late 1960s and early 1970s, i.e. attained a privileged position during the period of 'stagnation'. Those who had laid the foundation for further advancement at an earlier time reaped the harvest of social recognition during the period when the Soviet industry was grinding to a halt. It is no coincidence that when they are asked to name the best times in the country's recent history, Russian citizens invariably point to the 'stagnation era' that charted a peaceful course towards what is now known as the collapse of the Soviet state.

Stagnation Generation

The label for this generation is conditional. Its entry into an employment career coincided with the onset of a period of reform that culminated in the transition to market economy starting in 1992. In other words, the stagnation generation could not reap any benefits of the stagnation period, but rather had to face economic hardship and other problems flowing from Gorbachev's and Yeltsin's reforms. Nevertheless, at the point of entry most of them had to come to terms with the old Soviet system and its institutions of mobility.

The stagnation generation, now aged between 35 and 50, reached the age of 25 at the end of the stagnation period in the early 1990s. This was a generation with the highest level of education ever known to Russia. At the point of entry into the labour market, over 17 per cent sought and found white-collar employment, a significant leap upward compared to the previous generation for which the corresponding figure was just over 10 per cent. At the same time there was a smaller proportion of those who came to be employed in technical or clerical positions. The proportion of workers also showed a marked decline compared to the previous period, as did the proportion of farmers. The private entrepreneur – a totally new species for post-Soviet society – continued to gain ground. These trends point to the new conditions emerging in Russian society: declining industries and more white-collar employment in the private sector, and a profound crisis in agriculture that was losing the support of the state.

Table 6
The stagnation generation: structure of positions at 25 and 35 (%)

Position	Aged 25	Aged 35
Top manager	0.6	0.5
Mid-manager	1.3	1.5
Shopfloor manager	5.6	5.6
Private entrepreneur	0.1	0.8
Specialist	17.1	17.4
Clerk or technician	29.31	29.1
Worker	34.9	33.8
Farmer	1.4	1.8
Total	100.0	100.0

Let us now take a look at how individual careers fared in this period. One in four mid-managers had to find employment as a specialist or even a technician. The numbers in the position of shopfloor manager clearly declined: only 50 per cent of those who started out shopfloor managers held on to that position until age 35. Most incumbents declined into groups with no managerial control, a minority rose to become either middle or top manager. Significantly, a minority of shopfloor managers responded to the crisis by venturing into private entrepreneurship. The group of specialists also showed signs of prevailing downward mobility: 11.8 per cent of those who started their career as specialists had to come to terms with the position of clerk or technician, and 4.4 per cent with the position of worker. In the previous generation, the number of specialists going down to occupy working class positions was only 1.1 per cent. Clerks and technicians moved both ways, upward towards the position of manager and downward to the position of worker. Workers found themselves in a truly dead-end situation: the proportion of shopfloor manager positions was reduced and at the same time worker access to higher societal positions also declined. Farmers proved to be a very mobile group. However, their favourite channel of mobility (joining the working class in big cities) was also partially blocked. The mobility index (ratio of upward to downward mobility cases) came to down to 1.12.

Table 7
Stagnation generation: social change between 25 and 35 (%)

	Occupation at 35								Group Total
Occupation at 25	Top man	Midman	Shpflr man	Entrepr	Spclst	Clerk/ techn	Work- er	Farm- er	%
Top manager	20.0	20.0	0.0	0.0	0.0	40.0	20.0	0.0	100.0
Midmanager	10.0	50.0	0.0	0.0	10.0	30.0	0.0	0.0	100.0
Shopfloor manager	2.3	6.8	50.0	4.5	11.4	18.2	6.8	0.0	100.0
Private entrepreneur	0.0	0.0	0.0	100.0	0.0	0.0	0.0	0.0	100.0
Specialist	0.7	2.9	5.9	1.5	72.8	11.8	4.4	0.0	100.0
Clerk or technician	0.0	5.4	2.7	0.0	6.3	73.5	11.2	0.9	100.0
Worker	0.0	1.8	2.5	0.4	1.8	7.9	84.1	1.4	100.0
Farmer	0.0	0.0	8.3	0.0	0.0	25.0	8.3	58.3	100.0
Group total	0.6	4.2	6.2	0.8	17.5	30.8	38.0	1.8	100.0

It seems that a two-tiered mobility pattern is now evolving in Russia. The first tier is occupied by a group that can be called the actual and potential elite, comprising white-collar specialists and managers. In the new situation of a selective distribution of life chances, these people maintain privileged access to new institutions and channels of mobility: elite education, entrepreneurial managerial positions, big company hierarchies. The second tier is mostly occupied by the working class and farmers. Workers, disorganized and unexperienced in defending their rights, have lost the privileges they enjoyed in Soviet society. As we have seen, the position of worker implied an inherent chance for upward mobility, even though that was limited to the position of shopfloor manager or technician. There were only few workers who covered the distance that separated them from the group of specialists or mid-managers. Nevertheless, for their offspring there did remain the chance of mobility. In the new situation they are reduced to the position of an inferior class with no significant outlets to other, more advanced social groups. The data above can be regarded as a basis for further speculation concerning the emergence of a class society in Russia, with all the concomitant complications: class consciousness, class struggle, perennial instability. Let us now move on to take a closer look at mobility patterns of another kind, i.e. change of workplace.

Social Mobility in the Transition Period

The first years of transition brought no major changes to the Russian occupational structure (Chernish, 1994). Despite a profound crisis in industries, the majority of Russians remained in their former social positions. A variety of motives supported occupational conservatism. Firstly, large numbers of Russians firmly believed that the ongoing crisis would soon be over and that eventually things would return to the pre-1992 situation. Secondly, those who moved into better-paid jobs in the private sector often sought to keep their former status and preferred to continue to be called 'workers', 'engineers' or 'scientists' rather than 'small retail traders' or 'small scale entrepreneurs'. Thirdly, for many workers there was an obvious motive to hold on their former jobs since they were better defined in the law and entailed more privileges in case of retirement or job loss. However, structural change, though slow and inconsistent, continued to exert its pressure on the Russian labour force.

Change of Workplace

It is clear from the data that the five years of social change from 1993 to 1998 implied a fairly high level of social mobility. Firstly, the ageing of the population and the growing numbers out of work caused a not unexpected slide from the category of employed towards the non-working category. The reasons for this were as follows.

Table 8
Reasons for being out of work

	N	%
Retired	610	51.9
Disability	79	6.7
Child care leave	62	5.3
Long leave without a salary	11	0.9
Unemployment	231	19.7
Housewife	68	5.8
Student	77	6.6
Other reason	37	3.1
Total	1175	100.0

It is notable that the proportion of people out of work now constitutes one-fifth of the non-working category and about 10 per cent of the whole Russian population. In fact, the rate of unemployment might be even higher if we took into account the growth of the housewife category: this category has more than doubled in size during the past five years. There is reason to suspect that at least for some of the new housewives, their status was the result of their being easy targets for job cuts in the labour market.

Five Years Ago

High-ranking managers tend to quit their jobs for retirement reasons. Shopfloor managers appear to have been affected by redundancies much more frequently than other managerial categories. For white-collar workers with credentials, retirement and unemployment were also the strongest reasons to leave. However, close to one-third of the women in the group lost their jobs as a result of child care leave. Between 1993 and 1997 child care leave was a favourite strategy for educated women to quit the labour market with as limited adverse effects to their well-being as possible. Socialist child care legislation that stipulated benefits and that forced employers to keep the jobs of women on maternity leave, was still in effect. In view of imminent redundancies, some white-collar women chose to acquire the status of young mother and in this way freeze their employment situation for the next three years, hoping that the labour market situation would improve in the meantime.

Table 9
Reasons to change jobs according to former occupation (%)

	Occupation five years ago								Gr tot
	Top man	Mid-man	Shpflr man	Private entrepr	Spclst	Clerk/ techn	Work-er	Farm-er	%
Lost my former job	0.0	14.3	28.3	0.0	17.4	25.1	31.2	31.6	26.3
Found a job with a higher salary	0.0	10.7	8.7	0.0	17.4	7.9	12.5	0.0	11.1
Found a job with better employment of my skills	0.0	0.0	0.0	66.7	2.8	2.9	1.2	0.0	2.1
Found a job with better labour relations	0.0	3.6	0.0	0.0	1.8	0.4	0.0	0.0	0.5
Changed my place of residence	0.0	3.6	8.7	0.0	12.8	10.9	7.2	5.3	9.0
Found a job with better working conditions	0.0	3.6	2.2	0.0	1.8	4.6	1.2	10.5	2.7
Found a job with a better work schedule	0.0	3.6	0.0	0.0	4.6	1.7	1.2	0.0	1.8
Did it on the insistence of my relatives	0.0	0.0	0.0	0.0	0.9	0.8	0.6	5.3	0.8
Quit my former job through retirement	100.0	28.6	23.9	0.0	21.1	22.6	28.0	36.8	25.4
My company disintegrated	0.0	3.6	6.5	33.3	0.9	2.5	1.9	5.3	2.5
Dismissed because company cannot pay salary	0.0	0.0	0.0	0.0	0.9	0.0	0.3	0.0	0.3
Had to accept a long leave without a salary	0.0	0.0	0.0	0.0	0.0	0.8	0.6	0.0	0.5
Found a job with a more stable salary	0.0	3.6	0.0	0.0	0.0	0.0	0.0	0.0	0.1
Was transferred on the order of superiors	0.0	0.0	0.0	0.0	0.0	1.3	0.3	0.0	0.5
Enrolled in an institute	0.0	0.0	0.0	0.0	0.0	0.4	0.0	0.0	0.1
Conflict with my superiors	0.0	3.6	0.0	0.0	0.0	0.4	0.6	0.0	0.5
Maternity leave from main job	0.0	0.0	2.2	0.0	5.5	2.9	1.2	0.0	2.3
Personal reasons, family circumstances	0.0	0.0	0.0	0.0	0.9	0.4	0.0	5.3	0.4
Had problems with health	0.0	0.0	0.0	0.0	0.0	1.3	0.6	0.0	0.7
Quit my job for ideological reasons	0.0	3.6	0.0	0.0	0.0	0.0	0.3	0.0	0.3
Dismissed for job conditions violation, accident	0.0	0.0	0.0	0.0	0.0	0.0	0.3	0.0	0.1
Stayed at home as a housewife	0.0	0.0	0.0	0.0	0.9	0.4	0.3	0.0	0.4
Decided to stop working	0.0	0.0	0.0	0.0	0.0	0.8	0.6	0.0	0.5
Completed military service	0.0	0.0	0.0	0.0	0.0	0.4	0.0	0.0	0.1
My organization was sold to another owner	0.0	3.6	0.0	0.0	0.0	0.0	0.0	0.0	0.1
	100.0	100.0	100.0	100.0	100.0	100.0	100.0	100.0	100.0

White-collar employees without credentials seemed to choose the same strategy. They were more often than the previous category affected by unemployment and their response was similar. Workers seemed to be the main victim of the economic crisis and the mass unemployment that followed. There were fewer of those among them who voluntarily retired from their jobs and more than in other categories of those who had to come to terms with being made redundant. Farmers retired more often than other categories for obvious reasons: the rural population depleted by the outflow of young people in previous years is far older than other groups.

Among those who were still working in 1998, 57.9 per cent held the same jobs as five years previously, 26.7 per cent had to change jobs and 15.3 per cent did not have any job in 1993, mostly because they were new arrivals in the labour market. The fact that the majority kept the same jobs did not mean that there was no change. The same job respondents were invited to evaluate various aspects of change in their workplace in the past five years using a three-point scale, with '1' indicating there was a change for the worse, '2' no change and '3' implying a change for the better.

Table 10
Changes in job characteristics (adjusted mean of a 3-point scale for the group having the same jobs)

Job characteristic	Adjusted mean
Possibility to use skills	1.98
Relations between employees and managers	1.90
Promotion prospects	1.74
Technical sophistication	1.58
Social benefits	1.43
Salary level	1.39

There was very little change as far as the prospects of using one's skills were concerned. The relations between employees and managers changed for the worse, albeit only marginally. All other characteristics saw a dramatic change for the worse. As expected, technical sophistication decreased as a result of ageing machinery. Salary levels dropped even more dramatically. Social benefits associated with the workplace often ceased to exist altogether.

The new job respondents quoted three main reasons for changing their workplace: loss of job (26.3 per cent), finding a job with better pay (22.2 per cent) and change of place of residence (13.8 per cent). The evaluation of new workplace characteristics was not very different from the 'same job' category.

Table 11
Proportion of users of workplace benefits 10 years ago and in 1998 (%)

Social benefits	1988	1998
Provision of housing	24.5	1.9
Kindergarten	39.9	9.5
Beneficial holidays	52.3	12.8
Meals at workplace	19.6	5.3
Work clothes	42.3	31.4
Travel to and from workplace (costs covered)	11.2	7.8
Foodstuffs provision	9.5	2.5
Consumption goods provision	7.7	0.6

Table 12
Evaluation of new workplace characteristics

Job characteristic	Adjusted mean
Relations between managers and employees	2.02
Salary level	1.91
Possibility to use skills	1.89
Promotion prospects	1.76
Technical sophistication	1.75
Social benefits	1.54

Most of those who changed jobs did not lose out in terms of their salary. They also felt that relations between managers and employees were almost unchanged. However, the characteristics of the workplace itself came were not as good as five years previously. The change of workplace did not prevent reduced promotion prospects, a lower level of technical sophistication and much smaller social benefits.

In most cases the mobility vector pointed downward to less favourable working conditions, less machinery sophistication, less safety and fewer social benefits. The change of workplace made little difference since the same tendencies occurred in most Russian industries and agriculture.

Social Mobility Ideal and the Reality

High social mobility remains one of the goals of the reform process. However, the fulfilment of mobility dreams is still not associated with individual initiative. Below is the estimate of the influence of factors that may be conducive to worldly success at two points in time: ten years ago and in 1998.

Table 13
Estimate of importance of mobility conditions (mean on a seven point scale, 1 – unimportant, 7 – very important)

Quality	Mean		
	1988	**1998**	**Difference**
Rich parents	4.57	6.65	2.08
Relatives in managerial positions	5.32	6.59	1.27
Good education	6.21	5.55	-0.66
Useful contacts	5.76	6.71	0.95
Hard work	6.10	5.25	-0.85
Perseverance	6.05	5.84	-0.21
Ability to take risks	4.55	6.05	1.50
Ambition	5.25	5.44	0.19
Natural intellect	6.20	5.66	-0.54
Living in the capital	3.59	4.60	1.01
Right nationality	2.66	3.75	1.09
Foreign contacts	2.68	5.45	2.77
Charm, social qualities	5.23	5.57	0.34
Appropriate political views	5.37	3.61	-1.76
Honesty	5.44	3.73	-1.71
Law abidance	5.54	3.63	-1.91
Independence	4.44	4.91	0.47
Luck	5.67	6.17	0.50

It seems that popular assessments of the conditions for success have changed very dramatically during the past ten years. Firstly, personal and family ties have gained considerably in importance compared to the previous period: rich parents, relatives in managerial positions and useful contacts now play a key role in securing social advancement. Contacts also used to be important ten years ago, and therefore the difference is not as great as in the case of other conditions. However, the factor that gained more influence than others was having foreign contacts, obvious proof of the openness of new Russia. The conditions that lost most in influence were political affiliation, law abidance and honesty. The Russian populace obviously believes that during the past ten years Russian society has kept drifting away from the meritocratic principles of social selection towards a more subjectivized situation where parental contacts and relatives in important positions mean much more than individual excellence. Oddly, the old totalitarian system is regarded as a more balanced one, attaching more importance to natural intellect and good education.

Let us now explore which of the groups harbours greater *resentment* caused by the loss of some meritocratic principles. We constructed a 'meritocracy' index that is a ratio of values designating the importance of kinship ties and useful contacts and scores of importance attached to personal achievement such as natural intellect, hard work, ambition and perseverance.[1]

Table 14
Means and standard deviation for the meritocracy index

Occupation now	Mean	SD
Specialist	1.4846	1.2337
Clerk or technician	1.3364	1.0391
Worker	1.3154	0.7628
Mid-manager	1.2314	0.4220
Shopfloor manager	1.1931	0.3662
Farmer	1.1714	0.3029
Private entrepreneur	1.1291	0.2869
Total	1.3382	0.9196

It seems that all groups recognize the prevalence of networking and parental protection over individual qualities in the struggle for the attainment of privileged positions. Specialists with a higher education seem to have a less favourable assessment of the new Russian situation than others. However, the large standard deviation points to an obvious polarization within the group. This polarization can be traced back to a gap in living standards between various white-collar worker groups. The new Russian middle class, however small, has benefited from new conditions and is inclined to regard it more favourably. Entrepreneurs, though agreeing to a dominance of non-meritocratic qualities, place more emphasis on individual qualities than any other group.

In most cases then Russian citizens regard contemporary Russian society as lacking in basic social justice and meritocracy. Their response to the new situation consists in backing social forces that support a stronger state. Leaning on their past experience, Russian citizens know that a stronger state can be a balance to a web of informal ties that controls most social and material resources. There is an anticipation that ultimately, the weak Russian state will regain its clout and impose mobility patterns that might favour the underdog in the reform process. The call for state interference works as a self-fulfilling prophecy with more and more state intrusion into private life. However, the

[1] The formula for the index is as follows: $(\Sigma \text{ var } Si)/(\Sigma \text{ var } Ii)$ where 'var S' are variables denoting subjective contacts (rich parents, managerial relatives, useful contacts, contacts abroad) and 'var I' individual qualities. The index is greater than one if the contacts are regarded as more important. It is smaller than one if personal achievement is viewed as paramount.

question remains as to whether the new Russian state, fully controlled by the nouveaux-riches, will be able to perform the function of ultimate arbiter of individual achievement and work as a channel of mobility for the alienated groups.

Chapter 3

Labour Markets in Semi-Market Society

Jouko Nikula

Introduction

Advocates and critics of Soviet-type socialism have both characterized the Soviet Union as a dictatorship of the proletariat. What this meant, in practical terms, was that the employment authorities made sure each and every citizen in the country had a job – even though the individual rarely had much say about where that job would be. With the collapse of socialism it was widely expected that the previous limitations with respect to choice of work, working conditions, pay levels and other issues would soon be removed and that 'normal' labour markets would begin to evolve. As it has turned out, the reality lies somewhere in-between these two poles: Socialism was not a watertight system that afforded complete control over one's destiny in the labour market, but there also existed unofficial markets which allowed for freer movement of labour in and between jobs. The collapse of the socialist system has not completely done away with the former structures, but some of them have remained in place, albeit in modified form. This chapter discusses the development of the Russian labour markets with special reference to the following questions:

1) What are the main segments of the labour market: is the distinction between a core (*kadrovyi*) and marginal workers the main dividing line, or are workers possibly divided along other lines as well?
2) What are the main channels of employment: individual, informal or official?
3) What is the role of secondary employment in economic survival?
4) How do the private and the state sector differ from each other with respect to labour market situations, i.e. in terms of employment, wages, employment security, career advancement, etc.?

The Soviet Workplace

In the Soviet Union the workplace was very much the focus of social life: it provided not only employment, but also various fringe benefits that were extremely important to the daily life of the Soviet worker: kindergartens, schools, housing, holidays, shops, etc. Indeed it is easy to agree with Simon Clarke (1998, 2), who says that it was not the desire of the authorities to keep control over workers as such, that allocation and career advancement was planned, but to maintain social integration in society. The Soviet workplace represented a kind of mini-community or a second home for workers. It was very much a question of social status and stability: if you did not have a permanent job, you were branded as a social misfit, both in the eyes of your neighbours and friends and in the eyes of the authorities.

In the Soviet system the principal means applied in the competition for labour force was benefits; in that sense there were only very few restrictions on the movement of labour force. The main avenue of recruitment, apart from official employment offices, consisted of informal contacts between workers and management. It was quite common for several generations of the same family to go and work for the same company: sons followed their fathers in their occupational careers.

Many of these structures started eroding with the collapse of socialism, forcing companies to drop their social benefits: the provision of benefits now became the responsibility of municipalities. Having said that, benefits do still play a role in the recruitment of labour, especially in the case of skilled workers. In the private sector in particular, the most important means in the recruitment of skilled labour is pay.

Segmented We Stand?

Clarke and Kabalina (1997, 39) say that it is possible to identify three types of labour market in contemporary Russia: internal, unofficial and external. The first of these operates within the company and is based on the reallocation of existing labour. Unofficial markets are the main routes of recruitment to a new job and a second job. Here, social networks and relations are important; indeed without references it is extremely hard to get a job. The external or official labour markets are for those who are too old or unskilled for the internal or unofficial markets.

According to Clarke and Kabalina (1997, 42), the labour force consists of four segments: the core segment and the industrial, professional and peripheral segment. The first of these comprises highly skilled workers who are at the centre of social relations within the company. Their skills are company-specific and they have acquired these skills on the job. The industrial segment, then, consists of workers with a relatively low level of skills. Their value lies in their loyalty to the company, since they have been working for the company for a long time. The professional segment consists of workers with high skills but low loyalty to the firm, and employers are keen to compete for those workers. Finally, the marginal segment is characterized by low skills and low loyalty: these workers tend to float from one job to another.

		LEVEL OF SKILLS	
		high	low
LOYALTY	high	core	industrial
	low	professional	marginal

Figure 1
Segments of labour

The status of these segments differs within the company, as do their capabilities to act in the labour market. Core workers are capable of defending their position and limiting entrance from the outside. On the other hand, since their skills are company-specific and since they often are older, they have limited prospects for promotion.

Workers representing the industrial segment have acquired their position during a lengthy career in the company and through their loyalty to management. Their occupational mobility is rather low because they have limited chances to work elsewhere. The segment consists mainly of women, especially in clerical and auxiliary jobs.

The professional segment possesses the strongest position on the external labour markets, even though previously they were paid less than the core segment because of the nature of their work, which mainly consisted of auxiliary tasks. Nowadays their position is under threat from a major reorganization of managerial hierarchies and tasks. The peripheral segment is the most unstable group because of their high occupational mobility and low work morale. They frequently change jobs to get better pay (Clarke 1997, 42–5).

The position of workers and the type of labour market are not dependent on the strategies of management, but more on the company's financial situation. Companies that receive state subsidies and that operate in an export sector are in a far stronger position than those operating in a domestic sector without state support. These factors determine the quality of the company's labour force. Successful companies can attract highly skilled workers and pay them decent wages and offer them good social benefits. This very much helps management in their most important task, which is to keep the core of a labour collective intact and guarantee its reproduction (Clarke 1997). Companies that fail to do this will lose the best part of their work force and have to employ less skilled and more unstable workers. Over time this will lead to the erosion of the work collective, its skills and commitment.

Grosfeld et al. (1999) offer a different interpretation of the forms and types of labour segmentation. They argue that there are two segments of labour in Russia based on 'uncertainty and workers' heterogeneity and risk aversion' (Grosfeld et al. 1999, 1). The first segment consists of least productive workers, who will remain in the firm, even with their very low wages, as long as their social benefits are guaranteed. The second segment consists of workers who are more productive and who choose to leave low-performing firms and move to better-performing firms. In a sense this argument comes quite close to the views of Clarke et al. (1998) who say that there are two categories of employees, those who are afraid to leave and those who leave because of their awareness of external opportunities. Grosfeld et al. (ibid., 4) argue that these two segments can coexist even in the same firm, and both in private and state-owned firms.

Grosfeld et al. (1999, 4) have an interesting theoretical interpretation of the dynamics of the Russian labour market. According to them firms offer their workers a contract with low wages but guaranteed benefits: workers can either approve or reject that contract on the basis of their knowledge about their 'productive characteristics'.

The Russian labour force is clearly divided according to training and skills, with managers and professionals representing the most educated and skilled groups. These groups also show the greatest willingness and preparedness to continue with their training, professionals being far more willing than managers or any other group. Professional workers also think that their job tasks do not correspond to their training: most professional workers believe that their training clearly exceeds the requirements of the job.

Although the general level of education is relatively high, there are significant differences in terms of the scope of occupational training and its applicability to current conditions. For example, a clear minority of unskilled workers – as defined on the basis of an occupational classification – have received any occupational training. The same concerns female operators and clerical workers. In these groups assessments of the match between the requirements of the job and training were the lowest, with more than one in four saying that their training was not adequate in comparison with the requirements of the job.

Female managers, unskilled workers and a large part of female operators have had the least success in maintaining their skills. At the other end of the scale we have professional workers: in this group occupational training is very prevalent, assessments of the correspondence between training and job requirements are very positive, and professional workers have also had the most success in maintaining their skills.

Table 1
Education according to occupational groups (%)

	Mana-gers	Profs	Cleric-al	Craft	Operat-ors	Un-skilled	Total
Primary	–	–	1	4	2	9	2
General secondary	5	2	18	24	40	44	21
Specialized secondary	41	26	59	66	50	42	48
Higher	54	72	22	6	8	6	29
Received occupat training	67	67	44	48	54	31	51
Total	100	100	100	100	100	100	100
N	110	267	382	172	224	140	1300

Table 2
Correspondence of occupational training to a) requirements* of work and to b) work profile by occupation and gender (%)**

Occupation	Men		Women		Total	
	Re-quire	Profile	Re-quire	Profile	Re-quire	Profile
Managers	67	30	69	27	68	28
Professionals	66	10	70	7	69	9
Clericals	74	40	69	29	70	35
Craft	65	35	45	36	62	36
Operators	79	26	50	34	75	30
Unskilled	57	49	36	56	44	33

* occupational training is in line with the requirements of work.
** occupational training corresponds to work profile.

Most female and male workers think their training is adequate to meet the formal requirements of their job, while only a clear minority believe their training exactly corresponds to the requirements of their current job. The lowest level of satisfaction in this respect is shown by professionals, who as noted above have been most successful in maintaining their skills. This dissatisfaction is clearly associated with the financial situation of the workplace: the majority of professionals (81%) working in the state sector and two in three respondents in the state sector described the financial situation of their workplace as poor or very poor.

It is clear then that large numbers of professionals are working in jobs for which they do not have the right training. The Soviet system produced huge numbers of specialists, engineers, technicians, accountants and others who have now lost their previous jobs or whose training is somewhat outdated for the present job. When asked why they thought they had lost their skills, the most common reason identified by the respondents was that their present main job was not in line with their training; the second most important reason was the abnormal situation in the workplace, i.e. workers were unable to do their job because of the lack of cash, loss of markets or substandard of equipment. In this situation workers have no other option but to commit themselves to various auxiliary jobs such as cleaning, maintenance tasks, etc.

If we take our respondents' assessment of the financial situation in their workplace as a criterion for dividing them into segments, we find that a part of clerical and skilled workers in industry and trade, predominantly in the private sector, form a special niche of successful or dynamic workers. Workers in financially successful workplaces have better wages than others, they have less wage arrears and they work part-time less often. It has to be noted, of course, that employees' assessment of their workplace's financial situation is a rather dubious criterion, since lower management and employees do not necessarily have a very clear and accurate picture of the true situation in the company.

An important aspect of the differentiation of Russian labour markets has to do with regional differences. Ongoing economic reforms have mainly benefited Moscow and some other larger cities, but outside these central areas the effects of transformation have remained less visible. Our results indicate that in this respect, Russia can be roughly divided into three segments. The first, 'modern segment' is represented by Moscow and St. Petersburg, showing many of the features of dynamism that Grosfeld et al. refer to. These include such features as:

- a relatively low level of wage arrears,
- a relatively large proportion of firms with a solid financial situation,
- relatively high rates of job changes and
- a higher proportion of fixed-term labour contracts.

The second group consists of big and medium-sized cities, where the opposite is almost universally true. Small cities and rural villages represent the third group, where the situation is in many respects much worse.

Table 3
Features of labour market situation by place of residence (%)

	Mos-cow	St. Ptrsb	Big cities	Med. cities	Small cities	Villa-ges
Wage arrears	33	45	54	6 5	74	93
Same job as five yrs ago	48	46	65	53	62	58
Good financial situation of the firm	20	15	17	11	5	3
Fixed term-labour contracts	21	30	14	13	9	4

Labour on the Move

According to Grosfeld et al., workers with the best skills and the best training, i.e. with the most cultural capital that can be traded for better and more secure wages and interesting jobs, are those who are most likely to change jobs. Our results, however, lend support to the interpretation of Clarke and Kabalina: the most skilled workers with the best training are least willing to change jobs, because they represent the core of the labour collective. More than two-thirds of managers and professionals are in the same job as they were five years previously. Among skilled manual workers and clerical workers the share is clearly lower: just over half in these groups have remained in the same jobs.

Occupational mobility has varied according to the size of place of residence: in metropolitan areas over half of the workers have changed jobs during the past five years, while in smaller cities and rural areas this share has been around one-third. This of course reflects the better labour market situation in bigger cities and the wider range of choice.

As was pointed out above, the 'norm' in socialism was to have a job for a lifetime – even though it was possible to change jobs if one wanted better benefits. Labour mobility has now increased in present-day Russia, although most employees still work in the same workplace as five years ago. Mobility is lowest in the primary sector, in transport and industry, where two workers in three had the same job as five years previously. The number of mobile workers is highest in trade, where only one in three remained in their previous job.

Young workers living in Moscow or St.Petersburg showed the highest level of mobility, and workers in the private sector were more mobile than workers in the state sector. Managers and professionals had changed jobs because they wanted better wages, while clerical workers as well as semi-skilled and non-skilled workers had not had much choice: they had had to change jobs after having lost their previous job. Change of place of residence was another relatively common reason for changing jobs. For professionals, the main reason for changing jobs was poor working conditions: schedules, the possibility to apply one's skills and general working conditions. These accounted for one-third of all reasons to change jobs. Though professionals are least satisfied in their possibilities to apply their skills in their present job or in working conditions overall, they have nonetheless been the least mobile: only one-fifth of them have changed jobs. The reason lies either in the fact that their skills are not 'tradable' in other sectors of the economy, or that they feel so secure in their current position that there is no need for them to change jobs. Another relatively stable group is that of operators, who are well paid and highly skilled workers and therefore greatly valued by the companies. Among those who had changed jobs, the most important motive was better pay. Craft workers and clerical workers are both part of the industrial segment, they are more mobile than operators but less mobile than unskilled workers: for them the main reason for changing jobs has been losing their previous job. Unskilled workers clearly represent a marginal segment in terms of mobility: every other unskilled worker had changed jobs during the past five years mainly because they had lost their previous job.

Table 4
Reason for changing jobs by occupation (%)

	Mana-gers	Profs	Cleric	Craft	Operat-ors	Un-skilled	Total
Lost my job	7	4	37	33	27	42	29
Got job with better wages	35	28	19	22	33	7	22
Changed place of residence	10	20	14	16	15	9	9
Got a job with better working conditions	6	32	10	8	6	13	14
Other	24	10	7	15	6	14	11
N	29	50	93	55	48	71	346

Networks and Patrons – Ways of Getting a Job?

In the Soviet era social networks were a crucial part of people's everyday life. Through these networks they learned about goods that were hard to come by, and they were also a precondition for advancement in many respects; for getting into university, for getting a better apartment, etc. (Srubar 1991). From another angle, Soviet society has been described as clientelist: at all levels of

Soviet society there was a system of reference in place, meaning that you always needed a patron to promote your interests and causes.

The labour collective was one such system – 'a primary unit of Soviet society', as Simon Clarke (1993, 7) has noted. It was the manager's responsibility to guarantee the reproduction of the labour collective: his job was to provide the necessary resources to his collective, the labour, money, social benefits, etc. For workers, then, the labour collective provided not only a job but also social benefits, goods, health care and other necessities.

The beginning of transformation from planned economy to some sort of market economy has not rendered these practices futile, but the reproduction of the labour collective remains the major task for managers: to make sure there is a skilled and committed labour force in place, but also to look after the continuity of subsidies, orders, etc. The fact that there are two major routes to labour attests to the existence of internal and informal labour markets: appointment by superiors and with the help of friends and relatives. Appointment by superiors was typical of managers and professional workers, while help from friends and relatives was more common among lower white-collar employees and semi- and low-skilled workers. The third route is represented by personal activity and initiative. Official channels such as employment offices or newspapers were an option only for a minority: some five per cent of the respondents had found their job through an employment office, less than one per cent through a newspaper advertisement. Internal labour recruitment was more typical in state-owned companies (28 vs. 12%), while help from social networks was more important in the private sector (25 vs. 34%).

Table 5
Ways of getting a new job by occupation (%)

	Managers	Profs	Cleric	Craft	Operators	Unskilled	Total
Appointed	58	33	20	13	18	16	25
Proposed myself	9	23	27	45	43	39	31
Friends & relatives helped	17	23	36	28	26	31	28
Employer found me	8	12	8	6	6	4	8
Other	8	9	9	8	7	9	8
Total	100	100	100	100	100	100	100
N	110	265	370	166	220	140	1271

Despite the sharp decline in the influence and membership of Russian trade unions and the rapid growth of the private sector, we will not necessarily see an increase in part-time employment or atypical labour relations. In virtually all sectors the norm is a permanent job: around 90 per cent of all employees have a permanent job. In trade the share is markedly lower at 46 per cent. Fixed-term contracts (20%) and oral agreements (22%) are common. If we look at the forms of labour contracts in different age groups and regions, we find that young workers in Moscow and St. Petersburg in particular have predominantly fixed-term labour contracts. However, in contrast to the findings of Heinrich et al. (1997), we saw no predominance of fixed labour contracts or oral agreements among older groups. Temporary employment occurs primarily among young workers in trade and private services (catering, etc.). Outside Moscow and St. Petersburg, permanent jobs are the norm in all age groups and in all industrial branches. This is probably due to the lack of real employment alternatives in places where the local economy and labour markets is dominated by one major company. This is no doubt also the reason for the low mobility of the labour force and for the low level of civil unrest despite the problems with being paid on time.

They Pretend to Pay and We Pretend to Go to Work

One of the most intriguing features of Russian transformation has been the non-payment of wages. In developed capitalism the relationship between employer and employee normally assumes a contractual form, freely entered by both employer and employee: the labourer receives a wage in return for putting him or herself at the employer's disposal, and the employer usually pays the employee's wages according to the contractual terms (see Clarke 1998).

The Russian version of capitalism differs from the 'norm', however, even though there is the appropriate legislation in place and even though there is a formally powerful trade union movement with extensive powers. Nevertheless wage arrears have become a recurring feature of Russian working life. According to surveys by VCIOM, less than half the working population in Russians had received their wages in full. Regional variation in this respect is quite considerable: in northwestern parts of the country 63 per cent of the workers had been paid full, in northern areas the figure was much lower at 29 per cent (www.cspp.strath.ac.uk/SE2-Wages.delay-1.html).

In our survey 71 per cent of the respondents who were in the active labour force said they had not always been paid on time. Arrears were most common in the primary sector (mining) and in public services (health care, education) and relatively uncommon in private services such as banking, business services and trade and catering. The mean delay was six months, the longest delay being recorded in the primary sector at 18 months.

Table 6
Wage arrears by sector (%)

Sector	Wage arrears (%)	Mean delay (months)	Mean wage (Rbl)
Primary	88	16.0	503
Industry	73	5.0	1046
Transport	63	4.5	1121
Private services	29	3.9	1176
Public services	79	4.1	746
Administration	77	5.3	811
Total	70	6.1	896

Wage arrears concerned all occupational groups and both men and women. There were practically no differences between age groups and different levels of skill and training.

In small cities and rural areas wage arrears are almost three times as common as they are in Moscow, in St. Petersburg they are almost twice as common as in Moscow. In all areas wage arrears occur far more often in the primary sector and industry than in other branches. People working in trade and private services experience wage delays least often.

Forms of Redundancy

Although Russia has experienced dramatic economic decline since the beginning of reforms in 1992, this has not translated into high unemployment or led to significant civil unrest. The low unemployment rates are explained by the astonishing flexibility of the Russian labour force: people have continued to work even though they have not been paid and even though they have had to work part-time, accept various forms of administrative leave, etc. According to Clarke (1998, 8), enterprises succeed in retaining labour because they need it and because the costs of doing that are so low.

In our survey some 20 per cent of the labour force were out of work or working part time; a typical case is a middle-aged professional in public services who has a secondary specialized education and who lives in a small city.

The private sector does not offer safer employment than the public sector: the proportion of private sector employees out of work was nine per cent compared to five per cent in the public sector, while the proportions working part time were 17 and 12 per cent, respectively. However, it seems that neither sector favours the option of dismissal, either temporary or indefinite: only 2–3 per cent of workers had been dismissed on administrative leave during the past year.

Table 7
Percentage of workers in atypical employment

	%		%
City		**Industrial branch**	
Moscow	7	Primary	4
St.Petersburg	5	Industry	14
Big cities	9	Transport	9
Medium-sized cities	22	Private services	4
Small cities	38	Public services	10
Villages	29	Administration	10

Although the official unemployment rate stands at almost 20 per cent, although most respondents had been paid late and although industrial production has continued to decline, relatively few workers had suffered from negative consequences. It is also noteworthy that the negative consequences had affected all social groups quite evenly. In one of his recent articles Simon Clarke asks 'Do Russian Households Have Survival Strategies?' He argues that:

> the idea of a household survival strategy distracts attention from the principal sources of household subsistence, which are waged employment and social transfers. We have now seen that subsistence production and engagement in the informal economy make only a marginal contribution to household survival.

Clarke shows that most Russians cope mainly by normal means, wages (when they get paid) and social transfers (no matter how meagre). This contradicts common beliefs about ways of coping, which underlines the role of plot farming and various forms of social networks and casual work.

However, at times of temporary need, the most common forms of coping were help from relatives and friends and land-plots. In larger cities like Moscow and St. Petersburg, people resorted to more 'urban' forms of coping, such as casual work and living on one's savings. Land-plots represented the main source of livelihood in small cities and rural villages, but friends and relatives played a very crucial role here, too (see Blom's article in this volume).

Second Job – A Way of Coping?

The stereotypical view of life in post-socialist society has it that in order to survive in the harsh economic reality, people need to have more than one job. However, as Simon Clarke notes, there is considerable disagreement about the scale of secondary employment. According to estimates by the Russian Tax Inspectorate, 35–40 per cent of the adult population have second jobs.

According to Simon Clarke et al.:

> second jobs are not primarily the means by which the destitute survive: those in the best position in the primary labour market are also in the best position in the market for second jobs: men, the young, the more educated, those in larger cities, those working in the private sector and those in senior management and specialist posts are more likely to have a second job, to work longer hours in it, and to earn more from it.

Moreover, the share of those with more than one job is only 5 per cent of the adult population, for the rest a second job is not a real possibility, owing either to a lack of interest or lack of opportunities. Our survey confirms the conclusions of Clarke et al., showing that only a small minority of respondents had second job and that a second job was more common among well-educated, middle-aged residents of Moscow and St. Petersburg than among low-skilled, young or old residents of smaller cities or villagers. Second jobs were more common among those who had been unemployed, put on administrative leave or who were working part-time.

Among those who had a second job, 40 per cent were professionals and specialists, almost one-third skilled workers and only 10 per cent unskilled workers. Among managers and non-manual workers the proportions were very low. Most of those who had a second job worked in the same occupation as they did in their main job, for example three professionals out of four worked as a professional in their second job, 70 per cent of skilled workers worked as skilled workers and more than half of the unskilled workers worked in the same profession as they did in their main job. Examined from the opposite angle, more than half of those with second jobs worked in professional or skilled worker occupations and more than one fifth in non-skilled occupations.

So again, one could agree with Clarke who argues that:

> work *po sovmestitel'stvu* is still the most common form, with one fifth of people doing their second job at their own place of work and about half those whose main job is as a waged employee do a second job which is a similar basic type of activity to their first, another quarter doing second jobs which do not require any skill. (Clarke 1999,15)

Second jobs were not, however, significant to economic survival: only some seven per cent of the economically active population had incomes from second jobs. Four respondents out of five had no income from second jobs.

However, two-thirds of those with second jobs said that incomes from these jobs were very important to them. The most important sources of income, apart from wages from one's main job, were pensions and other forms of social benefits (42%) and monetary help from friends and relatives (23%).

As observed earlier, plot farming was an important means of survival for those who had been unemployed, who had been made redundant or who worked part-time. Upon closer analysis, however, it seems that plot farming has been important to those people who had not been unemployed, who had not been made redundant and who had worked part time. It was an important source of income for those who had a relatively secure labour market position and therefore had the resources to invest in plot farming. In a regional analysis, plot farming, like help from relatives, was more important in small cities and villages than in big cities, which offer more possibilities for casual work, which usually is unregistered and part of the 'grey sector'.

Table 8
Means of survival by labour market situation (%)

	Un-empl	Un-empl	Fired	Fired	Part-time	Part-time
	Yes	No	Yes	No	Yes	No
Plot farming	48	63	49	59	64	50
Help from friends and relatives	51	45	51	46	46	49
Casual work	38	29	37	31	31	34
Small scale trading	13	3	10	6	4	11
Own savings	22	20	22	21	20	24
Employer's benefit	8	10	17	8	10	7
Benefits from local administration	15	5	22	6	6	16

Private Sector – Source of Ever Growing Employment and Well-Being?

Many western analysts argue that privatization of the economy has a wide range of benefits: it helps to increase the efficiency of corporate management, it boosts productivity, and contributes to a more sound system of initiative and more rewarding work.

From a strictly economic point of view all this is no doubt true: having real owners is more profitable for the economy than having a group of politically advanced insiders whose main interest is to make quick profits by siphoning assets. In Russia the contribution of the private sector to GDP has rapidly increased from no more than five per cent in 1990 to 70 per cent in 1995 (World Bank 1996).

The definition of the private sector in Russia is very much contested, with different sources giving widely differing estimates of its size. The main reason for this is that the private sector comprises both formerly state-owned and completely new firms. In former state-owned companies, both management and personnel have remained unchanged, and there has been only a formal change of ownership. Many of the completely new firms are micro-firms that provide employment mainly to the owner and one or two employees.

Our data indicate that the private sector accounts for around one-third of total employment in Russia. Five years ago, the corresponding proportion was less than one fifth. The share is biggest in trade and industry, smallest in public services and transport. It has been precisely the productive sector, manufacturing and certain extracting industries (e.g. oil and gas), that has had the most wanted companies and where insider privatization was the norm. In fact many of these firms are heavily dependent on state support even though they are formally private.

Table 9
Form of ownership by branch (%)

Industrial branch	State	Private	Don't know	Total
Primary	73	24	3	100
Industry	37	61	1	100
Transport & communications	68	28	4	100
Banking & trade	18	67	15	100
Public services	85	12	3	100
Leisure & media	84	16	–	100
Administration	90	10		100
Total	67	30	3	100
N	876	392	46	1314

Those who have moved from the state to the private sector have benefited more than those who have either remained in the state sector or who have remained in the private sector. The improvements have been clearest in terms of pay level, in other respects the changes have been more modest. In many respects the changes have in fact been for the worse, especially those who remained in the state sector and those who remained in the private sector felt that things were just as they had been five years ago – there had been no significant improvement, but nor had things changed for the worse. (See Chernish's article in this volume.)

Workers in the private sector enjoyed greater autonomy than workers in the state sector: one in four were free to decide when to come to work, when to leave, when to take a day off without loss of pay and what to do during the day. In the state sector the corresponding proportion was around 12 per cent. In contrast to their greater autonomy and higher wages, workers in the private sector are rarely members of trade unions: only seven per cent belong to the unions compared to 55 per cent in the state sector. This difference mainly has to do with firm size: on average firms in the state sector are bigger than they are in the private sector. On the other hand it does seem that the state sector is virtually the only stronghold of trade unions in present-day Russia.

The chronic shortage of cash in the state sector is clearly reflected in the proportion of workers who have been paid late: in the state sector the figure is 80 per cent, in the private sector 19 per cent. However, people do not regard wage arrears as the key problem for Russia, in fact it ranked only fourth in the list of most pressing problems. The list was headed by such issues as rising prices, rising unemployment and general economic crisis.

Table 10
Features of different forms of ownership

Main job: type of organization	No. of personnel in organization	Mean wage in roubles	Wage arrears (%)	Max. wage arrears (months)
State	927	776	80	5.8
Private	120	1401	19	6.2
Joint stock	8383	1005	74	6.6
Cooperative	258	538	80	8.5
Public	79	491	83	8.6
Don't know	345	491	22	5.6
Total	23 287	869	70	6.1

Men and Women in the Labour Markets

The gender structure of the Russian labour market today does not differ very radically from that in other countries: women tend to work more often in the state sector (69% compared to 56% for men), in services and clerical work, and their wages are clearly lower than those paid to men, even though their level of education is actually somewhat higher than that of men. Overall it seems that while women enjoyed relative parity with men in past training markets, they have certainly lost out in terms of the correspondence of their training with the requirements of their present job. Furthermore, there is a clear 'class division' within women in this regard: women in managerial and professional positions have succeeded in maintaining closer correspondence between training and job requirements, while a greater number of women at the lower end of the occupational structure feel that their training does not meet the requirements of the job.

The fact that most women work in public services as teachers, doctors, lower bureaucrats, etc. mean that their work is more stable, but low paid. The differences are particularly clear at the upper echelons of the occupational structure. While 85–90 per cent of women have a permanent job, the figure for men is 65–70 per cent. On other hand, women's wages are no more than 63 per cent of men's wages, i.e. men earn one-third more than women. Almost every third man in clerical and professional work has a fixed-term contract, meaning that his job is a temporary one.

In most post-socialist countries the proportion of women out of work has increased to a greater extent than the corresponding figure for men. Rukavishnikov (1999, 5) notes that the majority of all persons officially registered as unemployed and almost half of all people out of work are women. What exactly does this mean? One possible explanation is that men have better chances to engage in informal labour than women do because they have less responsibility for household chores. This, in turn, would mean that men do not register as unemployed as often as women do. Another possibility is that women represent a larger share of 'disposable' labour, performing auxiliary and low-skilled jobs.

Our data revealed no significant gender differences in the occurrence of unemployment, dismissals or part-time work. In Russia, as indeed in all countries, the threat of unemployment is more acute among less skilled white-collar and blue-collar occupations. The only clear difference is seen for the share of workers in part-time jobs: the number of female craft workers and operators working part time is twice as high as the corresponding figure for men. Manufacturing and transport are the two main industrial sectors where part-time employment is more common. Within these sectors it is again blue-collar workers who are affected most often.

Almost 60 per cent of both men and women were at the same workplace as five years previously. In other words there has been quite considerable turnover. For men the main reason for changing jobs was to get better pay, for women that they had lost their previous job. Men have tended to rely on themselves to a greater extent than women, who have turned to their social networks, i.e. friends and relatives. Internal labour markets have also been important for both genders.

Although most respondents had a pessimistic assessment of their financial situation and future, very few thought they would have any real chance of improving their situation and well-being by changing to a new job or occupation. Most respondents thought their best chance to improve their financial situation was to hold on to their present job and get a second job.

Table 11
Ways of improving financial situation by gender (%)

	Males	Females	Total
Get a better paid job	22	16	19
Improve skills	15	13	14
Change occupation	6	5	6
Get a second job	25	20	23
Start one's own business	5	2	4
N	645	672	1317

This confirms the interpretations by Clarke et al. and by Rukavishnikov that Russian workers are indeed extraordinarily flexible: no one is paying their wages yet they still choose to remain in their present job, partly because their benefits depend on seniority. Nevertheless it is hard to believe that Russian workers have any contract – implicit or explicit – with their employers in which they agree to 'sell' their wages against job security. Even though trade unions on Russia tend to be rather weak (despite their extensive formal rights), there is no reason to believe that Russian workers have any vested interest in 'safeguarding' the interests of their employers. It is cheaper for employers to recruit low-skilled workers to do odd jobs and keep them on the payroll even if they don't have the money to pay their wages on time – because the only option is to pay dearly to dismissed workers.

Conclusions

The Russian labour market still carries strong features of the near past: examples are provided by the predominance of internal labour recruitment and the key role of social networks in job hunting. Instrumental motivations are predominant in job changes, at least at the upper echelons of the occupational hierarchy. The need to preserve the labour collective is reflected in the low proportion of those who have been made redundant or worked part time. There are no significant differences between the state and private sector in terms of job security. Overall, experiences were very rare, and the prevalence of wage arrears in all industrial branches clearly highlights the exceptional flexibility of the Russian labour market. Second jobs do not represent a particular means of survival at times of non-payment, nor does plot farming: these appeared most typically among people in a strong labour market position, among skilled employees engaged in managerial or professional jobs and among those with the skills and monetary resources needed for second jobs and plot farming. For most people the overriding goal seems to be stability, which means they are inclined to hold on to their present job for as long as possible, even if they are not paid. Instead of jumping into the 'cold water' of the external labour markets, people prefer to try and find additional work or a new, better paid job while remaining in their present job. Our data lend some support to the thesis of labour market segmentation into a stagnant and a dynamic part. However, it has to be stressed that the dynamic part still represents only a fraction of all workers: the majority still belong to 'the stagnant' segment. The popular explanation for this stagnation is the continuation of the policy where firms that fail to generate a profit are supported from the public purse and at the same time provide welfare and other services.

A recent (but by no means particularly novel) proposal to help 'cure' the Russian economy has been put forward by American business analyst McKinsley. The idea is simple: new employment from expansion will outpace layoffs from productivity gains:

> Overall, output growth should exceed productivity growth in these sectors, resulting in employment growth, which is what happened in Poland.' Eventually, however, 'the worst problem will have to be faced – seven percent of the total workforce could be put out of work at heavy industry that should be closed or slimmed, and unemployment in one-industry towns will outstrip new job creation. (http://www.russiatoday.com/features.php3?id=102609).

One has to concede that much of this is true: the rules of the game should be made clear and transparent, not only in the economy but throughout society. Improvements are also needed in the predictability of laws and regulations. But what exactly does this proposal mean for individual employees, especially outside Moscow, St.Petersburg and a handful of other centres of relative prosperity? Not much; mainly a threat of increasing unemployment and insecurity. As long as Russian society remains in turmoil, there is little hope of substantial foreign investment, except perhaps in the oil and gas industry. There is little hope of domestic investment either, for the very same reason; 'The massive outflow of capital bears evidence that the institutional environment was inadequate to warrant the quality of public spending or to attract private sector capital.' (Laurila 1999, 4) Rates of investment have been negative throughout the previous decade, and it is only during the last year that there have been signs of domestic production starting to grow. The other side of the problem, and part of the solution to the problem, is the question of informal institutions, to which McKinley referred by calling for clearer rules. The country's extensive shadow economy, high levels of crime and corruption coupled with low confidence in official institutions and a high level of social anomie are indicative of an introverted society with very low levels of generalized trust. As Raiser (1999) and Kolodko (1999) have emphasized, the only way to get back onto a positive track of development is to establish a sufficient level of generalized trust. Many things must change before this can be achieved: employees must have guarantees that they will be paid in time, that they will continue to have a job tomorrow and next week, and firms must be able to know that they will be treated fairly and equally, without any system of favouritism.

Chapter 4

Change and Continuity in Russian Work Organization

Harri Melin

Introduction

The Soviet Union was in essence a huge communist modernization project in which one of the key aims was to transform this vast country from an agrarian into a modern industrial society within as short a space of time as possible. The whole economic system was geared to this overriding objective, which was to be achieved by expanding industrial production according to the guidelines laid down by the Communist Party. The basic collective actor in the process was the industrial enterprise, which was at once the basic atom of social life and social organizations.

The Soviet Union has often been described by Western commentators as a command economy: the means of production were owned by the state and every aspect of the economy was vertically organized, centrally coordinated and bureaucratically administered. Coercive rules and legal sanctions were imposed to make sure that there was total compliance on the part of organizations and individuals. These vertical arrangements were highly durable and institutionalised (see e.g. Kornai 1990, 103). The whole economic system was coordinated by central planning organs. In principle, everything was done according to annual plans.

Another interpretation offered of Soviet-type economies has been to suggest that these were based essentially on bargaining. A bargaining society is a network of constant negotiations starting from the highest political level and extending all the way to shopfloor bargaining. In the Soviet Union there was constant bargaining also between the official economy and the shadow economy. As far as economic relations were concerned, these negotiations were vertical rather than horizontal in nature. Theories of bargaining society (e.g. Kornai 1990, Littler 1984, Burawoy 1989) help us to understand the complexities of everyday life in state socialism. There was a constant shortage of labour as well as of investment and consumer goods. In many branches there was a chronic imbalance between production and consumption. When the administrative system for the allocation of consumer goods failed, there were no informal networks to take their place.

There are also other interpretations of the nature of the Soviet economic system, work organization and labour process. Official Soviet theory had it that production was based on scientific planning, and the work organization was based on 'one-man management' (Arakelian 1950). American sociologists said essentially the same thing by using military organizations as examples of the Soviet work organization. All operations of industrial enterprises were centrally coordinated. Annual production plans involved thousands of indicators, which then determined everyday operations.

In the Soviet manufacturing system responsibility for every aspect of the factory's operation rested with the general director, who was assisted by a deputy director and the main engineer. The duty of each worker was quite simply to put the plan into effect: on this hinged the factory's success and prosperity, and by the same token the prosperity of the surrounding community. If they succeeded in achieving the targets set, the workers and the factory would be allocated additional resources. The bonuses awarded served as the main incentive throughout the economic system: not only manufacturing industries but also services operated on the basis of the same principles. The Soviet ideology was that workers were engaged in a conscious project to build a better future for communism.

The Soviet understanding of the role of industrial management involved an inherent paradox. According to the notion of one-man management, managers held a position of real power and were supposed to make all decisions. On the other hand, managers were seen as an integral part of the machinery of industrial ministries.

According to bargaining society theory industrial workers had important power resources at their disposal. Factories struggled with a constant shortage of virtually everything: raw materials, machinery, spare parts and skilled labour. All this meant that workers had real control over the flow of production, which afforded them a secure economic position and relatively extensive job autonomy. They were genuinely 'masters in their own house'. In other words, managers and the Communist Party did not have quite as complete control over production and over the workers as has often been suggested.

There was uncertainty regarding all elements of the production process. This was the basis on which labour and management conducted their negotiations. In reality, management had much more limited power resources than the official rhetoric gave to understand (see Burawoy 1985, 159–63). This was the reason why shopfloor workers exercised power and autonomy over the labour process, also providing them with some opportunity for resistance (see Blom et al. 1989, 36–9).

The official Soviet approach leaned very heavily towards homogenizing the work situation of different occupational groups. Soviet sociologists showed in several studies that the development of technology, division of labour and work organizations means increasing social homogenization (e.g. Rutkevich 1984). Class-based differences were denied, but there were nonetheless certain social divisions, most notably on the dimensions of urban vs. rural, male vs. female, mental vs. physical and qualified vs. unqualified.

The assumption was that all these divisions would disappear with social progress. In the same vein, the official view was that the factory was an entirely homogenous unit: the interests of different occupational, ethnic or other social groups within factories counted for nothing. Simon Clarke and his colleagues conducted a series of studies into the Russian workplace during the 1990s, in which the main concern was with management and industry in Russia (e.g. Clarke et al. 1996, Clarke 1999c). The research programme so far has consisted of a series of case studies in different branches of the economy and in different regions of the country.

The project's results have been described in several reports and publications. They show, for example, that in many companies there have emerged both internal and external conflicts during the years of transformation. The main line of contradiction runs between the enterprise's labour collective on the one hand and the markets and the political environment, on the other. In most cases the labour collective has to struggle to survive in what is a hostile environment (politics and markets). This gives management an opportunity to repress conflicts unfolding from internal contradictions (Ilyin 1996).

In their most recent studies the project has focused on employment and labour contracts in the emerging private sector, which mainly comprises small-scale trade and services. It has also penetrated some branches of light industry and arts and crafts. The results so far indicate that employment relations in new private enterprises are far less formalized than they are in traditional enterprises. However, there is no evidence that new private enterprises display a higher degree of numerical flexibility than traditional enterprises do. No major differences have been observed between different types of enterprises in terms of their functional flexibility (Clarke 1999a, 1999b).

The former Soviet Union is often described in the Western literature as a huge monolith. The assumption is that there existed in the whole country a single, universal work organization and identical managerial strategies across the country. In spite of this different branches of the economy and different regions in the country had their own individual practices: instead of one, there were several factory regimes.

The Soviet system collapsed more than ten years ago. What has happened since then in the Russian workplace? How has the Russian work organization changed? The discussion below looks at the changes that have taken place in these respects between 1991 and 1998 (see Melin 1996). The main focus is on the changes that have occurred in the realms of autonomy and authority relations.

The Work Situation of Different Occupational Groups

In the preceding chapters we have examined the changes that have happened during the 1990s in the Russian class structure and in mobility patterns, using the class typology presented by E.O. Wright. The main result of these analyses was that Russian society has become proletarianized, the working class has grown in size and the middle strata have declined. What about classes and work; how does class situation compare with work situation in the Russian case?

The interplay of class and work has been the subject of countless studies in advanced capitalist countries. The main result of these studies suggests that there is a close correlation between class position and work situation: people occupying managerial positions are more likely to enjoy a strong economic position than are industrial workers.

In our earlier analyses of the relationship between class and work in the Soviet Union (Melin 1996, Nikula 1997), we found that in general structural terms, Russian society in the early 1990s was a typical industrialized country. On the other hand there were also certain systemic features that set Russia clearly apart from capitalist countries. However, it emerged quite clearly that in an analysis of working life, occupational groups are the most useful analytical units: they are more concrete categories than classes. In the discussion that follows we shall look at the changes that have happened in the structuration of the work situation of the main occupational groups in Russia during the 1990s. The groups analysed are as follows:

Managers
Professionals
Engineers and technicians
Clerical and sales workers
Craftsmen
Labourers

These six groups account for roughly 75 per cent of the economically active population in our two samples. The focus below is on the social characteristics (gender, age, education) and key elements of the work situation (incomes, autonomy, authority) of these occupational groups. The general question we have is this: is there a similar tendency towards proletarianization in the workplace as was seen in the case of the class structure?

What, then, is the relationship between class and occupation? Our analysis suggests that Russian managers today belong for the main part to the following occupational groups: managers, professionals and engineers. Some three-quarters of all managers fall into these three groups. Supervisors and experts are most typically professionals and clerks by occupation, with more than half falling into these two groups. Skilled workers are for the most part craftsmen, non-skilled workers are primarily labourers (see Appendix Table 1).

Table 1
Breakdown of occupations by class groups (%)

	Man	Prof	Eng	Cler	Craft	Lab	Tot
Managers	63	19	18	6	5	2	11
Supervisors	18	12	17	9	4	3	8
Experts	12	18	30	13	–	–	10
Skilled workers	7	51	36	12	91	–	30
Non-skilled workers	–	–	–	60	–	95	41
Total	100	100	100	100	100	100	100
(N)	57	191	84	343	173	269	1117

The occupational group of managers shows a relatively close fit with the class group of managers: over 90 per cent of all managers belong to core middle class groups. Among professionals, half are currently working as skilled labourers. Two-thirds of engineers occupy middle class positions, one-third work as skilled labourers. Among craftsmen over 90 per cent are in the class group of skilled workers. The same proportion of labourers fall in the group of non-skilled workers. Clerks and sales workers also belong to working class groups. Overall then, there is a fairly close correspondence in present-day Russia between class and occupation.

Social Composition of Occupational Groups

As our results on changes in the class structure have shown, Russian society has become proletarianized during the past decade or so. As far as the occupational structure is concerned what this means is that the share of white-collar positions has decreased and that of blue-collar positions increased. At the beginning of the 1990s managers, professionals and engineers accounted for almost half (44%) of the groups analysed. Today, these three groups represent less than one-third (30%).

The Russian labour markets are a rather peculiar mixture of old and new. Although the vast majority of employees formally work in private companies, two-thirds of all workers still say they are employed by the state; only just over

10 per cent say they are in the employ of a private business. One-fifth work for joint stock companies. Over four-fifths or 83 per cent of the respondents have permanent jobs, only one in ten has a fixed-term contract. It would seem that fixed-term contracts are more common among managerial groups than in working class groups.

The gender system in the Russian workplace is also changing. Under the socialist system women's participation in the labour force was at a much higher level than in advanced capitalist countries. Another important feature was that women had full-time jobs for the entire duration of their working careers. Since the collapse of the Soviet system the level of women's involvement in wage labour has declined, but the same is true for the male labour force as well.

The structural changes that have swept across the Russian economy and its labour markets have caused unemployment to increase. According to data published by the United Nations, nine per cent of women and 10 per cent of men were unemployed in Russia in 1997 (Unicef 1999). The same source indicates that women had lost no less than seven million jobs from 1990 to 1995, while men lost less than two million jobs. Our results suggest that about 10 per cent of the labour force was unemployed at the end of 1998.

In the Soviet system there prevailed a situation of formal gender equality; one of the first laws introduced by the communist regime was aimed at guaranteeing women equal rights. In practice, however, the labour markets were characterized by very strict gender-based segregation, both vertical and horizontal. Women occupied managerial positions less often than men, and were more often engaged in service jobs. In this respect socialist countries did not really differ very much from advanced capitalist countries.

In the early 1990s the gender-based occupational segregation in Russia followed largely the same pattern as in capitalist countries, although there were some differences. First of all Russia had less female managers and engineers than the average advanced capitalist country did. Secondly, women in the Soviet Union were engaged in industrial work far more often than women in the West.

In the late 1980s women accounted for almost half of all managers and for just over half of all engineers. The proportion of women in both these occupational groups has shown rapid growth. Even during the Soviet era most professionals were typically female. Today, the female majority has continued to grow: by now more than four in five professionals are women. On the other hand the share of male clerical workers has increased. It is also worth noting that the working class is more clearly male-dominated today than it was ten years ago.

Our empirical data indicate that the Russian labour markets are undergoing some very profound changes: only the future will tell the real meaning of these changes. In the meantime it is interesting to look at the nature of work in which women are engaged in new professional and engineering tasks; and to address the question of whether the power resources or economic rewards are similar for both sexes.

Table 2
Occupational groups by age, gender and education in 1991 and 1998 (%)

	Man		Prof		Eng		Cler		Craft		Lab	
	91	98	91	98	91	98	91	98	91	98	91	98
Total	13	5	19	17	12	8	20	31	19	15	17	24
Men	55	53	22	19	54	48	13	24	73	87	58	78
Women	45	47	78	81	46	52	87	76	27	13	42	22
Under 31	30	19	10	32	30	10	22	25	27	21	23	20
31–40	34	30	27	28	31	22	24	31	24	25	24	31
41–50	26	37	18	28	28	31	18	31	23	36	22	29
Over 50	21	23	23	14	31	25	33	11	32	16	34	15
Primary	3	2	4	–	2	1	19	8	25	9	34	10
S'cndary	39	31	39	30	36	38	69	72	68	84	64	83
Higher	58	67	66	70	63	60	12	20	7	6	2	7

In its evaluation of human resources there was a strong leaning in the Soviet system to favour tradition and experience. This meant that there were far more aged top politicians and famous artists than in Western capitalist countries. The situation was different with regard to managers and professionals. On the basis of our data from the early 1990s there were in fact quite large numbers of young specialists. Service workers and unskilled labourers, on the other hand, were relatively old. Especially in female-dominated clerical occupations there was a large proportion of workers over age 60 (see also Lane 1987).

Our data shed interesting new light on the age structure in Russia. Looking first at the middle class, it is clear that managerial groups are rapidly ageing and that the age structure among professionals is shifting towards the middle-aged. On the other hand, there are more young engineers than there were ten years ago. In the working class the most outstanding change is the increasing number of young workers. At the same time the numbers in the oldest age group have declined quite dramatically.

The Soviet Union had a highly advanced schooling system (see e.g. DeWitt 1961), giving access for virtually all people to vocational training. There were also mechanisms in place to promote higher education in the working population. Many universities had so-called workers' faculties that provided evening and distant learning courses for those who were in wage employment. At the beginning of the 1990s different occupational groups were roughly divided into two categories in terms of their educational level, i.e. those with a university education and those with a vocational training. More than half of both managers and professionals had a university degree. Secondary education was typical of working class groups.

During the 1990s the educational level in the Russian population has shown a general tendency to rise (cf. Melin 1996, 102–13). Our data indicate that the numbers with no more than primary education have been sharply declining. In the working class the share of those with a secondary education has increased, but there are also quite considerable numbers of those who have a university degree. On the reverse side of the coin these trends are of course also indicative of a waste of resources: the allocation of training and education does not match the requirements of the labour markets. Our results also point at evidence of increasing inequality in education: today it is much more difficult to enter university studies from a working class background than it was during the Soviet era. One of the problems is the rising cost of university studies: workers quite simply cannot afford to send their kids to universities.

Wages

In state socialism the factors that determined the class situation of social classes were different from the corresponding factors in capitalist countries. For instance, the relationship between incomes and social position was not determined by the same rules. In capitalism there is a tendency for both negative and positive aspects of the social position to accumulate, and education and incomes show a strong positive correlation. In the Soviet system this was not the case. A skilled industrial worker used to earn more than an expert with a high level of education (Wesolowski 1969, 128–32).

In the Soviet Union income differentials were not as wide as in advanced capitalist countries (see e.g. Nowe 1977, 208–11). This is clearly confirmed by our empirical data. At the beginning of the 1990s there were no significant differences between the working class and middle-class groups. Managers had the best incomes, but craftsmen earned as much as engineers and professionals. This was due to the special role of manufacturing industries on the one hand, and to gender-based labour market segmentation, on the other.

Table 3
Incomes by occupational groups and gender in 1991 and 1998 (all employees = 100)

	Man		Prof		Eng		Cler		Craft		Lab	
	91	98	91	98	91	98	91	98	91	98	91	98
Men	149	166	155	144	124	151	116	95	115	109	114	111
Women	97	128	84	92	96	84	67	70	87	85	73	67
Total	125	147	101	102	109	117	73	76	108	106	98	100

However there were clear differences between the wages of men and women in the Soviet system as well. These income differentials were largely in line with those seen in advanced capitalist countries. In particular, male professionals had much better wages than their female colleagues.

The income distribution in Russia has now been changing with the emergence of capitalism. One clear indication of this is the growth of income differences. Managers today earn considerably more than they did in the socialist era, at the same time the relative wages of skilled and unskilled labourers have tended to decline. It is also worth noting that the relative wages of professionals have come down.

What about the difference between the wages of men and women? The evidence from earlier research suggests that the gender gap in wages has changed very little since the collapse of the Soviet system. In 1997, women earned about 70 per cent of men's wages in Russia (Unicef 1999, 8). In Finland, women's wages were 79 per cent of men's wages in 1998 (www.stat.fi).

Our empirical evidence suggests that the wage gap between men and women has grown somewhat smaller during the 1990s. Indeed in certain respects it might be fair to say that women have emerged as winners from the battle for wages. In the light of our results the wage gap has decreased in virtually all occupational groups, but there are two important exceptions, i.e. engineers and labourers. In these two groups income differentials have increased. Especially in the groups of managers and professionals, men have been pulling away from women. Today, men's wages are in relative terms much better than they were ten years ago.

A clear majority of our respondents are not satisfied with how their incomes have developed. In the questionnaire they were asked how they saw the changes in wages and salaries during the past five years. Over half (61%) indicated their salary level had declined. One-fifth were of the opinion that there had been no change. Only 16 per cent said that their incomes had improved. These positive assessments were more common in managerial groups than among workers. Two-thirds of all non-skilled labourers said their wage level had come down.

Autonomy

One distinctive characteristic of the Soviet work organization was that workers enjoyed broad autonomy at work, much more so than workers in advanced capitalist countries. For instance, they enjoyed considerable flexibility in terms of their working hours and work practices, in spite of the presence of formal rules and norms. One explanation for this is that workers were forced to be autonomous. This 'forced work autonomy' was a consequence of the constant shortages suffered in raw materials, spare parts and maintenance services: there was no other option than to take control of tasks and responsibilities that were beyond their formal work tasks (Burawoy 1985, Blom et al. 1989). In other words, autonomy was not something the workers had achieved after bitter struggles, but quite simply dictated by the circumstances.

The work situation of managers and professionals in the Soviet system differed from that in Western countries, where managerial and professional groups usually enjoy relative autonomy in their work. It is commonly accepted that these groups can freely decide on their working hours, pace of work, schedules, etc. On the other hand, managers are loyal to their employers and they are expected to work long hours whenever that is required. The same applies to professionals. In the Soviet Union managers and professionals were also subject to the plan.

Table 4
Autonomy by occupations in 1991 and 1998 (can decide %)

	Man		Prof		Eng		Cler		Craft		Lab	
	91	98	91	98	91	98	91	98	91	98	91	98
When to leave job	3	59	26	17	21	7	20	11	13	9	22	7
To have a day off	9	49	26	18	31	20	27	15	24	12	18	10
To work a bit slower	3	61	62	50	68	33	48	34	46	28	37	20

At the beginning of the 1990s managerial and professional groups differed significantly from working class groups in terms of their autonomy: managerial groups had much more say about their own job than workers did. Overall our results contradict the notion of high work autonomy throughout the occupational structure (cf. Burawoy & Krotov 1992). Workers had less say about their working hours or pace of work than was assumed. On the other hand over one-fifth of the workers could decide when to leave their job, over one-third could decide to have a slow day if they wanted to.

Apart from the time aspect of job autonomy, to what extent were our respondents in a position to decide on what kind of products they worked with? Our results are indicative of very high levels of autonomy. Almost half or 47 per cent say they could largely determine the nature of the product. Managers have much greater autonomy on this dimension than labourers (60 vs. 34%). It is clear from these results that at least certain elements of old Soviet-type work autonomy are still in place.

One important aspect of work organization is the question of the strenuousness of work. Research from the Soviet era suggests that workers had quite flexible work arrangements and did not experience very much stress on the job. What about the situation today?

Table 5
The physical and mental strenuousness of work according to occupational group (%)

	Job is always physically stressful	Job is always mentally stressful
Managers	39	48
Engineers	42	46
Professionals	30	45
Craftsmen	45	32
Labourers	58	21

Today the evidence suggests that experiences of stress at the workplace correlate closely with occupational position. Managerial groups indicate that their job is quite often mentally tiring, while working class groups say more often that their job is physically demanding.

It emerges quite clearly from our findings that the Russian work organization is in flux: it seems that the 'standard' pattern of capitalist organization is gaining ever more ground in Russia as well. Managers have seen an increase in their autonomy, at the same time as other groups have seen their autonomy decrease. This applies most particularly to engineers and workers. Over half of the respondents said that during the past five years they had seen no changes in the prospects of applying their skills and knowledge. Almost one-quarter (22%) said their prospects had decreased. Among managers the corresponding proportion was over 35 per cent. Overall it seems that management is trying to gain firmer control over other occupational groups. The subordination of workers to managerial prerogative is an ongoing process in contemporary Russian working life. The calls for greater efficiency and performance are clearly now affecting the shopfloor level.

Authority and Decision-Making

In the Soviet Union about one-quarter of all employees were in managerial or supervisory positions. In this respect the state socialist system was quite similar to the capitalist economy. The same applies to the gender division of managerial work: the majority of all managers and supervisors were men. During the 1980s Soviet sociologists were engaged in a programme aimed at promoting changes in shopfloor work organization, which were to be achieved by increasing the use of work teams and by dismantling traditional hierarchic structures. The idea was to employ 'work brigades', which were supposed to have almost complete autonomy to decide upon the division of labour and incentives in the brigade (see e.g. Andreyenkova 1985, 129–35). However this project never really got off the ground, but management in Soviet enterprises remained firmly grounded in old practices.

The position of Soviet industrial managers was based on their expert knowledge and their formal position in the industrial organization. David Lane has described them as 'constitutional leaders' (Lane 1985, 22). The operational field of managers was also influenced by the Communist Party, the government and trade unions. The Party was responsible for political questions, the government was in charge of matters related to production and the trade union focused on welfare aspects.

In a recent account Sheila Puffer (1996, 18) has described red executives as 'micro managers' and 'macro puppets': in everything they did their aim was to grease the wheels of the state. Puffer is sharply critical of enterprise management during the Soviet era, arguing that managers lacked the power resources they would have needed.

In the Soviet models managers had (at least in theory) no say in decisions concerning the volume of production or such aspects as 'marketing'; these were issues that were decided in the framework of the plan. However, they were in charge of everyday business. They also had an important role in local elites together with party officials and top bureaucrats; they represented economic elites in local circles.

Table 6
Supervisory power by occupation in 1991 and 1998 (%)*

	Man		Prof		Eng		Cler		Craft		Lab	
	91	98	91	98	91	98	91	98	91	98	91	98
Supervisory position	85	77	24	27	32	28	15	12	16	8	7	6
Work tasks	89	79	76	24	87	30	72	12	86	7	63	4
Work load	86	71	83	29	91	29	70	18	79	7	63	4
Pay rise	71	57	34	15	50	15	24	6	28	3	10	1

* The question concerning supervision and authority was divided into two parts. First, the respondents were asked whether in their job they supervised the work of others. Second, they were asked whether they were directly responsible for certain aspects concerning subordinates' work.

The Soviet Union was an industrial society. At a certain structural level modern industrial organizations were quite similar in both capitalist and socialist countries. For instance, in the early 1990s the number of employees in managerial and supervisory positions was roughly the same in Finland and in the Soviet Union; in fact socialist work organizations employed somewhat more managerial staff than capitalist work organizations.

In the early 1990s Russian engineers occupied managerial positions less often than their Western colleagues. In Finland, for instance, the majority of engineers occupy managerial positions in the formal hierarchy and have subordinates. In the Soviet Union engineers were most typically employed as experts. The situation was the exact opposite with certain clerical and craftsmen duties. In the Soviet Union these occupational groups had occupational authority more often than the same groups in Finland.

All workers in supervisory positions had considerable influence over the daily work of their subordinates (at least according to self-report). In the Soviet Union large numbers of workers in working class positions indicated they had authority positions. This is not the case in capitalist countries. One explanation is provided by the work that was done in brigades, which had extensive autonomy, including influence over the work organization and even wages. If you worked in a brigade as an informal supervisor, that meant you also had supervisory power (see Blom et al. 1991, 356). The second reason was that in the Soviet Union, industrial workers traditionally held a special position: the industrial working class was the most important force in building the future communist society, which meant they enjoyed certain special privileges.

In the Soviet Union there was a clear difference between male and female participation in organizational decision-making: men occupied positions of decision-making authority three times more often as women. Women managers usually occupied positions at the lower end of occupational hierarchies. Managerial practices were heavily male-dominated, in spite of the official rhetoric of gender equality.

The system began to change in the late 1990s with the adoption of the same practices and work organizations as are seen in capitalist countries. Managers are in charge of managerial duties, and other occupational groups have only marginal power resources in this respect.

Table 7
Decision-making (direct participation %)

	Man		Prof		Eng		Cler		Craft		Lab	
	91	98	91	98	91	98	91	98	91	98	91	98
Hiring or sacking	62	46	18	5	21	2	12	2	17	2	10	–
Budgeting	48	38	18	9	13	5	12	2	10	1	8	–

In practice all other occupational groups have lost their decision-making powers. Even in the early 1990s professionals and engineers had much less say in decision-making than managers, and by now the gap has grown even wider. Working class groups have lost all their power resources with respect to organizational decision-making.

Our analysis of the class structure in Russia today points in the same direction: decision-making powers are increasingly concentrated. The limits are set by economic needs and economic boundaries. In many everyday practices the Soviet system delegated its powers to the shopfloor level. Today, those who make the decisions are also responsible for those decisions and their consequences. The hard budget constraint has replaced the soft budget constraint.

Conclusions

What is happening in Russia today in respect of wage work? There are signs of both change and continuity. Working life in Russia today is characterized by profound changes as well as old traditions. Although the state socialist system collapsed ten years ago, many old institutions and practices are still in place. This is particularly true with regard to working life: the old work culture is still changing very slowly.

Simon Clarke and colleagues (e.g. Clarke and Kabalina 1994) have stressed that the main aim of managers during the transition period has been to retain their control over factories. Susan Linz (1997, 14) makes the same point by suggesting that 'the reality in Russia appears to be the maintenance of status quo'. Work collectives are still very much alive and an integral part of everyday life in factories.

But there are changes as well. At the macro level, Russian society has certainly been characterized in recent years by constant economic and political turbulence. Workers have experienced this turbulence in the form of unpaid wages or a decrease in real earnings. Income differences have increased, and managers are earning much more than they did during the Soviet era. Unemployment has also increased throughout the 1990s, and this is hitting the working class to a much greater extent than the middle class.

Women played a key role in the project to build socialist society. Today, women represent a huge potential resource for Russian society. However, much needs to be done if the problem of gender inequality is to be resolved. Russian labour markets are sharply segregated along gender lines, women continue to earn less than men and the majority of managers and supervisors are men. Women need support to promote entrepreneurship, and many barriers to upward mobility need to be removed. In particular, active steps are needed to increase the level of women's participation in the private sector.

There has been a clear tendency for work to become more and more intensified in Russia. All occupational groups feel they have lost part of their former autonomy. At the same time they have to work harder than before. Manager's decision-making powers and authority have increased, while those of workers have declined. Increasingly, decision-making power is concentrated in the hands of top management. Blue-collar workers simply follow the instructions and orders of their supervisors.

What, then, can we expect of the future? The class nature of contemporary Russian society is clearly seen in its working life as well. Our data lend strong support to the interpretation that working life in Russia is approximating Western practices. Old ideological aspects are receding, economic calculation is assuming ever greater importance. This means that the old unity of work collectives is coming under increasing pressure. Needs and interests are set to become more and more fragmented, meaning that certain segments within the working class are bound to emerge as winners while the broad masses will inevitably lose out with the profound changes that are going to take place in the near future.

Appendix

Table 1
Class and occupation (%)

	Mana-gers	Super-visors	Experts	Skilled workers	Non-skilled workers
Managers	30	11	6	1	–
Professionals	30	24	31	30	–
Engineers	12	15	22	9	–
Clerks and sales	17	32	40	13	45
Crafts	7	8	–	48	–
Labourers	5	10	–	–	55
Total	100	100	100	100	100
(N)	121	91	112	332	461

Chapter 5

Reproduction and Classes During Economic Crises

Raimo Blom

Transition, Labour Markets and Reproduction

The development of capitalist markets in post-socialist countries is having a major impact on the position of classes and social strata as well as on their opportunities for reproduction. At the same time the processes of transition are giving rise to increased social inequality and polarization.

One of the theories offered to explain how social stratification is affected by these processes is the market transition theory of stratification (see Nee 1989, 1991, 1996, Nee and Matthews 1996). The theory has been tested by Gerber and Hout (1998) in their studies of income development in Russia in 1991–95. The key propositions of the theory are that (1) market opportunities enhance returns to both education and entrepreneurial initiative; and (2) market transition diminishes the rentlike advantages that political elites derive from their redistributive power (Gerber and Hout 1998, 2).

The effects of transition are in many ways conditional. The progress of market economy may be hindered by various factors. For instance:

- transitional societies have a very unstable position in the international division of labour;
- the institutions required by modern market society and institutional regulation are still underdeveloped (Blom 1996, Brunetti et al. 1998);
- the democratic political system remains incomplete;
- civil society and the structures and channels of stable interest formation are lacking;
- modern mentality is still in the process of formation (Srubar 1991).

Successful economic transition requires the presence of established institutions to support the economic system. However, the necessary preconditions have not yet been met. For example:

- post-socialist countries do not yet have a mature regulation regime in place, which means that regulation is in many ways underdeveloped and deficient;
- the lack of social order that follows with the absence of a mature regulation regime implies insecurity as well as difficulties for people in establishing an action orientation; at the same time the pace of change is extremely fast, and there are conflicting norms between different institutional fields;
- there is a weak relationship between system integration and social integration (Lockwood 1966, Mouzelis 1991), causing problems of delegitimacy, anomie and social disorganisation.

Comparative studies indicate that the new positions formed in post-socialist societies are strictly hierarchic. For instance, before-after comparisons of occupational differences in reproduction and work situation between Estonia (in the Soviet and post-Soviet era) and Finland reveal dramatic changes and an opening up of wide differences between the top (managers) and bottom levels (workers) (Melin 1995).

Post-socialist transitional societies differ widely from one another at least in terms of their historical background, types of privatization, the emerging power structure and systems of social security. Both the levels of (under)development and the forms of societal transformation differ from case to case.

Post-socialist societies do not yet warrant the description of capitalist societies proper. This applies most notably to the Russian economy, which has been described as a form of 'merchant capitalism' where exchange between firms is based on barter (Burawoy and Krotkin 1994, Burawoy 1997). Privatized conglomerates still have autonomous actors based on the 'feudalization of state power'. As Burawoy says in a somewhat crude generalization, '(t)he mass of the population falls back into a primitive, intensified domestic economy of dachas and subsistence plots and trading and buying their wares in the thriving bazaar' (Burawoy 1997, 1442).

In contrast to the managerial capitalism that evolved in Central Europe, the process of transition in Russia has been described as being of the nomenklatura type. However, nomenklatura positions are of significance in many other post-socialist countries as well. The difference between the special case of Russia and these countries is highlighted by Eyal, Szelenyi and Townsley (1997), whose theory is linked up with 'new class' theories in an almost ironic way. Szelenyi and Konrad (1979) were the first to predict the rise of intellectuals to power in socialist countries as a scientific and human 'merger' between the bureaucratic estate and old intelligentsia.

Today, it is managers who are expected to rise from the dust of communism, to benefit most from the absence of a capitalist class and from the continuous need for information management. In the new situation that has unfolded since the collapse of communism, property relations are highly diffuse. The question of power is not about ownership, but about the control of productive assets. The authors argue that managerialism is a rational strategy in the present, unstable economic situation, which also serves to legitimize managerial claims for power. This legitimacy is provided by a constant 'problematization of uncertainty'. Managers, the authors continue, 'seem to be monopolistic owners of secret, almost mystical expertise'. The hegemonic ideology of managerialism is 'monetarism', which in effect is more than just an ideology; it is a political technology, a highly effective mode of governing individuals.

The hard core of the new power elite is represented by the technocracy and managers, who possess both cultural capital (monetarism), social capital (social networks) and economic capital (at least to a greater extent than other groups). In the class space (1997, Figure 2) the propertied classes are small entrepreneurs located somewhere in the middle. Sharing the same level as small employers, we find the category of white-collar workers, on the lowest level we have industrial and peasant workers.

The main coalition partners for managers are represented by the politocracy and intelligentsia (including the humanist intelligentsia, historians, sociologists, philosophers and playwrights).

The theory of managerial power proposed by Eyals and others comes close to the theory of professional groups emerging to power, and by the same token to the market transition theory of stratification. However, the theory is applicable not to the case of Russia but primarily to the post-socialist countries of Central Europe. In Russia, power is to a much greater extent about inheritance and connections – which provides a further argument against the market transition theory of stratification.

Compared to the situation in Central Europe the labour markets in Russia have shown some distinctive and peculiar features throughout the transition period. Data provided by the World Bank (though not fully reliable) suggest that the decline in real wages has been even sharper in Russia than in Central Europe, while the decrease in non-wage incomes and consumption has been lesser than the decrease in wages. Unemployment in Russia has not grown as sharply as in many other post-socialist countries, but the decline in employment exceeds unemployment growth much more clearly than in Central Europe. In November 1996 over nine per cent of the economically active population were unemployed according to ILO criteria; roughly the same proportion were forced to take 'administrative leave' during 1996 (Mellor 1999, 55).

Overall employment rates have been on the decline during the process of post-socialist transition. Between 1991 and 1996, the figures were at around the same level as in seven other transitional economies. Looking more closely at how the decline in employment rates breaks down, we can see that in the Russian case unemployment accounted for around six per cent and the change in participation in employment for about eight per cent (Gimpelson 2000, Table 1). The flow out of employment was biggest in the oldest age group, in the category of secondary education and among unskilled occupations. These differences are also very clear (Gimpelson 2000, Table 2).

There are reliability problems with all the figures available, as is clearly shown by Simon Clarke (1998) in a comparison of Goskomstat data and results from the Labour Force Survey and the Russian Longitudinal Monitoring Survey. Between 1990 and 1996, estimates for the decline in the employment rate ranged from 12 to 24 per cent.

Real incomes and purchasing power have been very much affected by the decline in production and hyperinflation. Between 1991 and 1995, the value of average real wages in Russia dropped by almost two-thirds (Gerber and Hout 1998, 21, Table 5).

Russia has also seen a very sharp increase in poverty, which ties in closely with unemployment. In 1993, 63 per cent of Russian households headed by an unemployed person were below the poverty line, while the figure for all households was 25 per cent. Number of children is another major factor associated with the incidence of poverty. In 1992, 46 per cent of Russian households with two children under age six were poor, and 85 per cent of households with three or more children were poor. Estimates of poverty also vary quite widely, but it seems clear that official data underestimate the rate of poverty (see Commander et al. 1997).

One of the factors with an impact on the development of labour markets is the nature of private enterprise. If the present situation of labour hoarding continues and if the informal sector continues to grow, as seems to be the case in Russia, then the potential for growth and for creating new vacancies is highly limited. The trend now has been towards increasing inequality. Commander and others (1997, 22) conclude:

> In short, the RLMS (= Russian Labour Marker Survey) data show that Russia entered the transition with significant inequality and this inequality has been magnified in the subsequent period. The decile ratio shows a very large increase over the period, at least when looking at per capita incomes. There were significant fluctuations in real income between rounds but taking the period from mid-1992 through the end of 1995, there was a clear decline of around 20 per cent. The decline was unevenly distributed. The lowest deciles experienced unambiguous declines in mean incomes and income share.

It has been estimated that the 'shadow' economy equals around 20–40 per cent of the size of the formal sector; some local surveys suggest it is even larger

(Mellor 1999, 54–5). Combine with this the extensive influence wielded by the mafia, the massive corruption at all levels of Russian society and the profound political instability and stagnation, and it is clear that Russia has not yet reached the state of mature capitalism.

The existence of different income sources or 'economies' is by definition against the ideal type of wage worker society. Rose (1991, 22–30) identifies three main groups of economies in which people in post-socialist countries participate: (1) official economy (legal, monetized), (2) social economies (legal, non-monetized; household production, reproductive networks of friends and relatives), and (3) uncivil economies (illegal, monetized; 'second economy').

In the discussion below we take a closer look at how the reproduction situation (incomes, need satisfaction) has changed in Russia. The data for the analysis come from two surveys carried out in 1991 and 1998 (see Social distinctions 1999).

The focus of the analysis is on questions of equality and the polarization of reproduction conditions. A further concern is with the question of modern wage worker society. In addition to the presence of normal capitalist society (production for profit and for capital accumulation of capital, separation of direct producers from the means of production), further conditions for the definition of wage worker society are (1) the dominance of wage labour relations in the (official) labour market, and (2) the sufficiency of wages as a means of reproduction for the majority of the population.

Classes, Strata and Reproduction

The general trend in Russian society today is towards increasing reproduction problems and increasing social inequality and polarization; this picture is confirmed by several studies (see e.g. Clarke 1999). For individual citizens this typically translates into the need to have more than one source of income (Rose 1993). The self-report results of our own survey show that the clear majority (79%) feel their well-being has declined, and most respondents believe this trend is set to continue. The picture is largely the same when we look at how people are spending their money: more of that money goes towards basic necessities (food, medicine) than before, and less is left for spending on major investments (car, housing), travel, leisure activities, even children's schooling.

So what, exactly, is the reproduction situation of different class groups and different categories of the economically non-active population? How do different resources relate to one another in the transformation of reproduction situations? To what extent does the market transition theory of stratification help us to understand reproduction situations? And what kind of overall societal system of reproduction is now taking shape?

The overall distribution of incomes is relatively skewed. A comparison of the distribution of individual and family incomes shows that in Russia, families are able, to some extent, to balance out the consequences of the transitions and income differences.

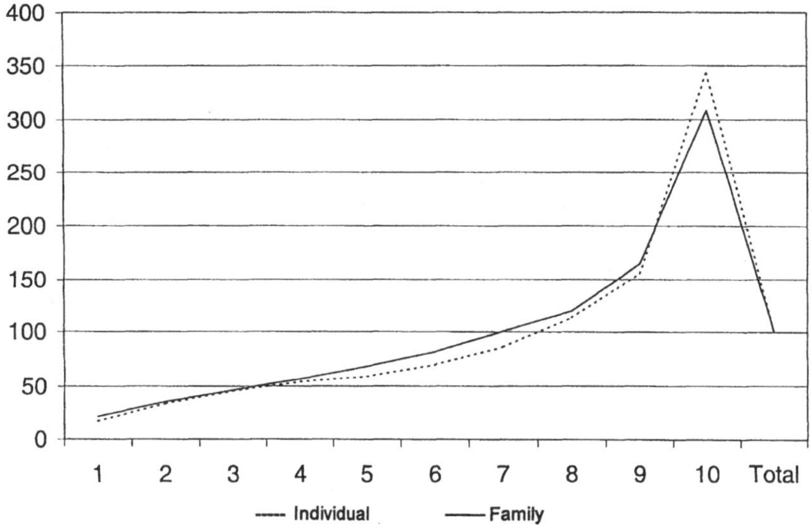

Figure 1
Distribution of individual and family income according to deciles (all=100)

The 1998 survey included several different items for the measurement of the level and problems of reproduction. The level/problems of need satisfaction were also measured by items concerning need satisfaction (to what extent do the resources available suffice). Over half of the respondents say it is difficult to find the money to buy clothes. Some 20 per cent do not have enough money to buy the food they need. This figure is rather lower than estimates published of the extent of poverty in Russian society. Over four-fifths or 86 per cent say it is difficult to find the money they would need to buy consumer durables.

The comparison of incomes and levels of need satisfaction also indicates that the need for extra money that would allow the step to the following level of need satisfaction increases level after level. In other words, the distance from food to clothes is quite short, but somewhat longer from clothes to durables and longer still from durables to more expensive investment goods.

Large numbers rely on more than just one source of income. One in five say they get extra from relatives or from pensions, eight per cent have a second job. There are some differences between class groups in terms of the importance of income sources. A second job is most important among managers (13%). Savings are more important in the group of self-employed than in others.

In the economically non-active population these factors are rank-ordered differently. The most important source of income here are pensions, followed by assistance from relatives and salaries. Help from relatives is extremely important for all groups except that of pensioners; it is most important of all in the group of students. Large numbers of students (38%) also have a job. Wages from main job are also important in the group of housewives (42%) and among those 'not working for other reasons' (46%). A second job is also very important for more than one in ten in the categories of unemployed, housewives and students. Small-scale retailing is important for one in ten among the unemployed and housewives.

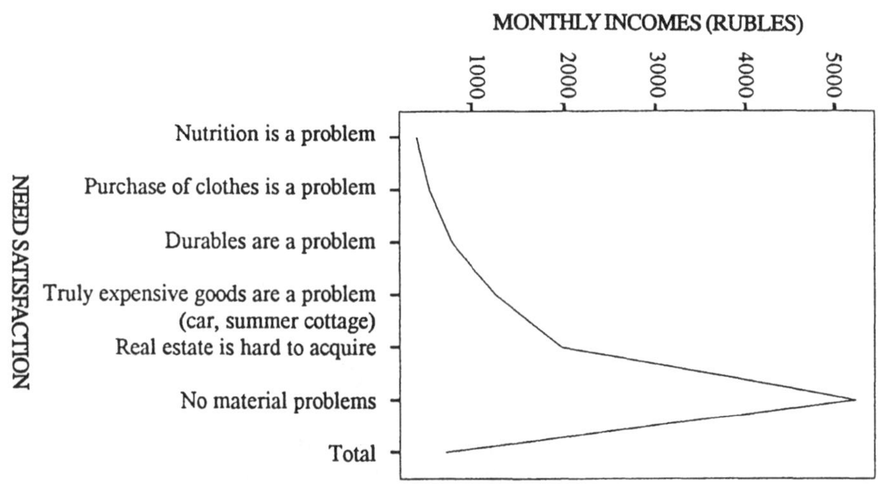

Figure 2
Incomes and need satisfaction

Table 1
State benefits by class (% recipients)

	Class variable Wright '97 (collapsed)						
State benefits	Self-employed	Manager	Supervisor	Expert	Skilled worker	Non-skilled worker	Total
Unemployment benefit	0	0	1	0	1	0	0.4
Child benefit	21	21	27	33	28	23	26
Housing payment rebate	3	19	20	12	17	11	14
Disability benefit	0	2	3	1	1	3	2
Other	0	2	2	0	4	4	3

Table 2
State benefits in economically non-active population (% recipients)

	Reason for not working					
State benefits	Retirement	Unemployment	Housewife	Student	Other reason	Total
Unemployment benefit	0	24	7	3	5	6
Child benefit	1	20	39	3	49	12
Housing payment rebate	43	10	13	7	9	29
Disability benefit	11	1	9	0	0	7
Other	8	1	6	14	3	6

As indicated by Tables 1 and 2, state benefits remain an important source of income, in spite of their small size. The most significant benefits are the child allowance and the housing benefit. The importance of these different benefits obviously varies between different classes and groups within the economically non-active population. The housing allowance is unimportant as far as the self-employed are concerned, but highly important to pensioners. One-quarter of the unemployed get unemployment benefit.

Table 3
Workplace benefits ten years ago, now and change according to class (% who had / who was)

Work-place benefits	Self-empl-oyed	Mana-ger	Super-visor	Expert	Skilled worker	Non-skilled worker	Total
Provision of housing							
10 yrs ago	8	33	22	17	21	17	20
Now	0	3	1	1	4	1	2
Change	–8	–30	–21	–16	–17	–16	–18
Kinder-garten							
10 yrs ago	24	38	38	35	36	34	35
Now	0	9	10	14	10	7	9
Change	–24	–29	–28	–21	–26	–27	–26
Beneficial vacations							
10 yrs ago	26	63	50	43	46	40	45
Now	0	20	20	17	12	7	12
Change	–26	–43	–30	–26	–34	–33	–33
Meals at workplace							
10 yrs ago	13	23	17	10	21	19	19
Now	0	9	8	6	6	5	6
Change	–13	–14	–9	–4	–15	–14	–13
Work clothes							
10 yrs ago	34	35	34	19	38	45	38
Now	8	23	33	17	35	33	30
Change	–26	–12	–1	–2	–3	–12	–8
Travel to and from work							
10 yrs ago	13	13	14	6	10	11	11
Now	3	9	15	11	8	6	8
Change	–10	–4	+1	+5	–2	–5	–3
Foodstuffs							
10 yrs ago	5	12	8	5	6	8	8
Now	0	2	5	2	2	3	2
Change	–5	–10	–3	–3	–4	–5	–6
Consump-tion goods							
10 yrs ago	3	10	7	4	6	6	6
Now	0	0	3	1	1	1	1
Change	–3	–10	–4	–3	–5	–5	–5

The Soviet workplace was a welfare structure in its own right that provided many different welfare services crucial to everyday reproduction. It was also a place of paternalistic domination and collectivism. Collectivism has not lost its significance during the transitional period, but it has been suggested that the relationship to the labour collective has continued to structure workers' behaviour during the changes. That is, the reaction of workers to the pressures of reform has exhibited both an attachment to collective institutions of the past and active development of individual survival strategies. The 'pressures of reform' include problems with wage payment, short time and administrative vacations, redundancies, tightened local labour markets, enterprises' divestiture of *sotkul'tbyt* and the general erosion of social support (Ashwin 1998, 195). Russian patience during the transitional period has also been interpreted from this perspective as a combination of alienated collectivism and individual survival strategies (ibid., 196).

In our survey we asked our respondents what benefits they had in their workplace ten years ago and today. All benefits have decreased and some are no longer available at all. The biggest losses have been experienced in housing services, kindergartens, vacations and meals. These changes have had both direct impacts on the reproduction of households and indirect effects through social relations. In this new situation individual survival strategies are necessary. The reduced significance of enterprise-level collectivity has also undermined the possibilities of worker mobilisation.

In sum, our results highlight the need for multiple sources of income. It also emerges clearly that help from relatives is extremely important to large numbers of people; somehow, they must compensate for the benefits they have lost. The picture we have drawn does not yet include the importance of garden plots to people; nor have we been able fully to assess the impacts of the long delays in being paid or in obtaining free housing and other services (see Mellor 1999).

In a survey at the height of the crisis at the end of 1996, it was estimated that as many as 65–7 million people in Russia had not received their wages, salaries or pensions on time on at least one occasion during the year (Russian Survey 1997, 5; Mellor 1999, 55). In July 1998, the total amount of wages overdue was 70 billion new roubles, equivalent to just over one month's pay for all wage earners in the whole of Russia (Clarke 1999, 114).

Transition and Russian Families

Social transformation and Russian economic crisis in 1998 have both had a major impact on the well-being of Russian individuals and Russian families. On average the whole population has experienced a change in their living conditions. The general standard of living has changed for the worse. On average more than four in five respondents say their well-being has declined since the late 1980s. Only six per cent indicate that their situation has improved.

Families have experienced the change in a similar way as individuals. The general comment is that well-being has declined if not collapsed:

Table 4
Change of well-being since 1988 in different families (%)

	Improved	Worsened
Managers	11	78
Professionals	10	83
Technicians	5	88
Clerks & service	6	86
Crafts	7	84
Operators	3	91
Not EAP	2	95

There are some differences in these experiences: manager families have somewhat fewer less experiences of decline and together with professional families clearly more positive experiences than other family types. Overall, however, the situation is very similar across all types. The vast majority of all families feel that the period of social transformation has thus far implied economic decline and that overall well-being has deteriorated considerably since the Soviet era.

In contemporary Russia it is often said that families cannot survive without the help and assistance of their relatives. What do our findings say about this?

Table 5
Assistance from relatives by family type (important %)

	%	No such assistance
Managers	20	66
Professionals	21	57
Technicians	27	55
Clerks & service	32	50
Crafts	28	52
Operators	25	62
Not EAP	24	65

Among people who live alone this assistance is clearly more important than among families. On average half of all people living alone say that everyday help from relatives is very important. Families do not differ very much in this respect: an estimate of the relevance of help from relatives varies in the range of

20–33 per cent. The figures are highest among clerk families and lowest among managers. On average one-quarter of all families say that help from relatives is very important to them. On the other hand, just over half of the families say they do not get such assistance.

Reproduction and Class Families

Differences in social reproduction and coping find expression in household and family differences. Households are in somewhat different positions with respect to their relative incomes, though the differences are not particularly wide: as measured by income indices, the differences between one-parent families and single households to two-parent families and singles living with relatives are between one-third and one-quarter. Relatives living in the same household have a different impact on incomes depending on the type of household. The situation appears to be the best for singles living with relatives (index = 106), the worst in one-parent families living with relatives (index = 72).

Table 6
Family income index (based on OECD consumption unit number)

Household type	Mean	N
Single	87	145
Single with relatives	100	415
Couple, no child, no relatives	101	445
Couple, no child, but relatives	100	382
One-parent family	80	63
One-parent family with relatives	72	36
Two-parent family	107	702
Two parent family with relatives	95	198
Total	100	2386

Family types	Mean	N
Couple: Manager	135	174
Couple: Professional	140	263
Couple: Technician or semi-professional	102	227
Couple: Clerk or service worker	97	173
Couple: Craft	91	173
Couple: Operator or elementary	81	221
Couple: Not EAP	75	433
Single parent	77	97
Total	99	1761

The above typology is based on occupations, with the highest position adopted in each case as the determinant for classification. In other words in a manager family, for instance, either both or one of the spouses occupies a managerial position. In a craft family, one of the spouses will occupy a craft position while the other spouse will be either in a craft or in a lower occupational position.

An examination of class families no doubt yields greater differences than one based on households. Families can be divided into three categories: 1) managerial and professional families (index = 135–40), 2) families of technicians or semi-professionals, clerks or service employees and craft workers (index = 91–102), and 3) families of operators or elementary workers and non-active population categories (index = 75–81). The first group of families represents the upper middle class, the second the lower middle class and the third the working class and underclass. Measured in terms of incomes, the first category of families earns almost twice as much as the third category.

We have seen that there are quite considerable regional differences in incomes and reproduction conditions. In the discussion that follows we move on to look at regional income differences by family types. The regional income differences can be detected within each family type. From managerial families through to families of the non-active population, income levels are clearly highest in the metropolitan areas, followed by cities, towns and finally rural villages. The regional differences are greatest in the case of managerial and professional families and smallest within families of the non-active population and single-parent families, with the index points ranging from around 150 through 100 (among the family types in-between) through to 50 points. The extent of the regional differences is obviously related to the income levels of family types. Managerial and professional families are bound to lose more than other families if they do not live in the metropolitan areas. On the other hand it is important to bear in mind that the prices of goods also vary regionally. Therefore the figures in our Table do to some extent exaggerate the differences in reproduction conditions.

There are also income differences by age, though these are less outstanding than the regional differences. In managerial families and in craft worker families, the oldest age group (over 55) have by far the best incomes. The same is true, though in a less pronounced manner, in families of technicians or semi-professionals, in operator families, in families of the non-active population and in single parent families. There are no clear age differences in professional families or in families of clerks or service workers, or these differences are in the opposite direction to those observed for other types of families.

Table 7
Type of settlement and incomes in different family types

Family types	Type of settlement	Mean	N
Couple: Manager	Moscow & St.Petersburg	229	23
	City	199	24
	Town	123	79
	Village	78	48
	Total	135	174
Couple: Professional	Moscow & St.Petersburg	213	39
	City	232	20
	Town	140	146
	Village	62	58
	Total	140	263
Couple: Technician or semi-profess.	Moscow & St.Petersburg	169	17
	City	119	29
	Town	104	123
	Village	69	58
	Total	102	227
Couple: Clerk of service worker	Moscow & St.Petersburg	150	16
	City	101	19
	Town	100	98
	Village	65	40
	Total	97	173
Couple: Craft	Moscow & St.Petersburg	148	21
	City	106	29
	Town	81	109
	Village	51	14
	Total	91	173
Couple: Operator or elementary	Moscow & St.Petersburg	160	25
	City	119	27
	Town	77	89
	Village	49	80
	Total	81	221
Couple: Not EAP	Moscow & St.Petersburg	117	38
	City	80	56
	Town	73	206
	Village	64	133
	Total	75	433
Single parent	Moscow & St.Petersburg	112	6
	City	87	6
	Town	72	64
	Village	76	21
	Total	77	97
Total	Moscow & St. Petersburg	168	185
	City	124	210
	Town	96	914
	Village	63	452
	Total	99	1761

Table 8
Age and incomes in different family types

Family types	Age	Mean	N
Couple: Manager	18-24	106	4
	25-39	126	53
	40-54	132	93
	55 or over	173	24
	Total	135	174
Couple: Professional	18-24	169	13
	25-39	130	107
	40-54	146	121
	55 or over	147	22
	Total	140	263
Couple: Technician or semi-professional	18-24	169	18
	25-39	119	93
	40-54	107	105
	55 or over	122	11
	Total	102	227
Couple: Clerk of service worker	18-24	115	20
	25-39	101	67
	40-54	85	71
	55 or over	108	15
	Total	97	173
Couple: Craft	18-24	70	20
	25-39	93	75
	40-54	80	58
	55 or over	136	20
	Total	91	173
Couple: Operator or elementary	18-24	80	19
	25-39	84	81
	40-54	75	89
	55 or over	91	32
	Total	81	221
Couple: Not EAP	28-24	66	10
	25-39	49	37
	40-54	53	40
	55 or over	81	346
	Total	75	433
Single parent	18-24	63	9
	25-39	74	57
	40-54	85	31
	Total	77	97
Total	18-24	96	113
	25-39	98	570
	40-54	104	608
	55 or over	93	470
	Total	99	1761

In sum then, we may say that class or occupational families differ in terms of their income levels, and that these differences are greater than those observed between household types. Regional differences are retained within family types. For obvious reasons they are greater in families at the highest level (among managerial and professional families), than in the families at the bottom (among non-active families and single parents). The differences in regional price levels can still be noticed in assessing the differences in reproduction conditions. The age differences with families are less pronounced than differences between regions. The most general case is that age increases family incomes, especially so in managerial and craft worker families.

Social Classes and Incomes

An examination of the incomes of different class groups in 1991 and 1998 by gender gives us a rough indication of how reproduction conditions have changed in Russia during the transitional period thus far. As Melin shows elsewhere in this volume, professional positions with managerial functions have benefited most from the changes, while managerial positions without a professional background (from technical, semi-professional, other occupational groups) have suffered most. Skilled workers have seen a small relative decrease in their incomes, while the group of non-skilled workers has seen no changes.

According to the double criteria of political and professional competence, the top positions in state socialism have seen a change in the situation and the market value of professional competence has increased. Nonetheless top incomes can only be earned in a managerial position.

Examined by class groups, the income structure in Russia today is strictly hierarchic. Workers earn about 45 per cent of the incomes of expert managers. By Western standards this is not yet a very large difference, however. The difference is biggest between the top two managerial groups and all middle-level class groups, and clear but less dramatic between the middle-level groups and workers.

In sum, our results are very much in line with the findings of Gerber and Hout (1998), contradicting the market transition theory of stratification changes.

The picture drawn above about social differentiation and polarization in Russian society needs to be heavily revised: 1) About half of the respondents in our data set are out of work; the number of those in gainful employment has dropped by some 15 per cent during the transition. 2) There are also some extremely rich people in Russian society who cannot be reached by our survey. It has been estimated that the new elite accounts for about one per cent of the total population (Bäckman 1998), a handful of them are in the category of super-rich.

Gender differences in income levels are wider than they are in the Nordic countries. Today women in Russia earn about 67 per cent of men's earnings. The gender income difference has slightly decreased from 1991 to 1998. The biggest relative changes have happened in the groups of experts (where the inequality has increased) and skilled managers (where the inequality has almost disappeared altogether). Income differentials have also grown in the category of top managers, among workers there have been no noteworthy changes.

Incomes in the economically non-active population are about 60 per cent of the figure for all respondents. In the non-active population the lowest level of income is recorded for students, the highest for pensioners. The analysis of family incomes shows that the situation is worst for the unemployed, while pensioners are the second lowest income group. At the family level, the incomes of students and housewives are clearly higher than in the other groups.

Table 9
Income indexes (all=100) in different categories of the economically non-active population

Reason for not working	Respondent's individual income index	Respondent's family income index
Retirement	64	72
Unemployment	58	68
Housewife	57	123
Student	43	140
Other reason	43	105
Total	60	82

The difference between the unemployed and pensioners and other groups in the economically non-active population can also be confirmed by examining the levels of need satisfaction in different categories. Over one-third of the unemployed and 29 per cent of pensioners have difficulty finding the money they need to buy enough food. In both groups 70 per cent indicate they do not have enough money to buy the clothes they need.

In sum, our analysis of incomes in the economically non-active population clearly highlights the problems of those who are no longer in gainful employment, particularly the unemployed and pensioners. In these particular categories, even relatives can do little to help improve these people's reproduction situation.

Table 10
Levels of need satisfaction in different categories of the economically non-active population (%)

	Reason for not working					
	Retire-ment	Un-empl	House-wife	Stu-dent	Other	Total
Nutrition is a problem	29	36	10	4	14	26
Purchase of clothes is a problem	43	35	29	33	37	40
Durables are a Problem	23	25	38	36	31	26
Expensive goods are a problem	5	3	23	27	18	8
Total	(690) 100	(231) 100	(69) 100	(73) 100	(111) 100	(1174) 100

Both age and type of settlement also have a clearly dividing effect on incomes. The highest incomes are recorded in the younger middle-aged groups, the lowest in the oldest and the youngest age groups.

Table 11
Respondent's income index and family income index by type of settlement

Type of settlement	Respondent's income index (mean)	Respondent's family income index (mean)
Moscow	179	173
St.Petersburg	172	190
City (pop. over 1 million)	107	106
City (pop. 500–999,000)	144	154
Town (pop. 100–499,000)	68	62
Town (pop.50–99,000)	103	104
Town (pop.10–49,000)	99	101
Town type settlement	81	75
Big village (more than 100 households)	65	65
Smaller village (fewer than 100 households)	65	55
Total	100 (2206)	100 (2399)

Examined by type of settlement, by far the highest levels of income are recorded in Moscow and in St. Petersburg, the lowest in rural areas. In the two major urban centres income levels are almost three times as high as in rural villages. However, the pattern is not entirely linear. In towns with a population of 100,000–499,000, the situation is almost as bad as in the countryside. In cities with a population of 500,000–1,000,000, people have relatively good incomes.

The relationship between education and incomes lies at the heart of transition theory, which has it that education and professionalism increase their influence in the (positive) distribution of rewards. We noted earlier that there has been a tendency in the class structure for professional groups with managerial functions to increase in size. Incomes increase with level of education, most dramatically so from the third to the highest level. This can also be clearly seen in the relationship between level of education and need satisfaction.

Table 12
Education and incomes (income index: all=100)

Highest educational level		Respondent's income index	Respondent's family income index
Primary	Mean	58.9	59.2
	N	296	301
General & unfinished secondary	Mean	76.3	87.2
	N	517	589
Secondary special & unfinished higher	Mean	96.8	97.1
	N	957	1056
Higher & academic	Mean	162.9	150.8
	N	436	453
Total	Mean	100.0	100.0
	N	2206	2399

Table 13
Education and incomes in 1991 and 1998 (all gainfully employed =100)

	Incomes	
Highest educational level	1991	1998
Primary	72.7	53.9
General or unfinished secondary	91.4	77.4
Secondary special or unfinished higher	91.5	88.2
Higher or academic	119.5	142.8
Total	100.0	100.0

The market transition theory of stratification predicts that educational qualifications assume increasing importance in economic rewards. The changes in Russia from 1991 to 1998 show that this has indeed been the case. The differences between educational levels are much greater today (89 index points) than they were in 1991 (47 index points). The difference has increased most between the two highest levels of education (from 28 index points in 1991 to 55 points in 1998).

The effect of education on incomes varies according to age group and place of residence. When we cross-tabulated three age groups (18–30, 31–50 and over 50) and region (three categories according to well-being of the region; mainly from Moscow and St. Petersburg to rural villages), the effect of education on incomes was highly differentiated. The joint effect is much greater in the middle-aged and older age groups in the metropolitan regions than in any other age/region category. In the age group 31–60, the difference in the income index (all = 100) between those with general secondary education or less and those with a higher education was 83 index points. The corresponding figure in the age group over 50 was 74 points. In the other two regional categories, the same effect of education varies from 0 to 36 index points according to age group. In the youngest age group in these two regional categories, the effect of education on incomes is minimal (only 0–11 index points). The variation in income differentials is related to the level of incomes in different regional categories. In the metropolitan regions, the total mean income was 214 points and in the two other regional categories 104 and 70 index points.

Table 14
Income index by occupation and managerial position (individual income index: employees=100)

Managerial position	Occupation	Mean	N
Managerial	Professionals	155	72
	Semi-professionals	93	55
	Other	148	164
	Total	140	288
No authority	Professionals	91	157
	Semi-professionals	72	144
	Other	88	644
	Total	86	945
Total	Professionals	111	229
	Semi-professionals	77	196
	Other	100	808
	Total	99	1233

Finally, we can try to differentiate the effects of education from both variables defining class position, i.e. authority and professionalism. Authority refers here to formal authority based on decision-making position. Professionalism and semi-professionalism are defined by occupations. Incomes are measured by an index where all employees = 100.

A professional position gives higher incomes. Semi-professionals have by far the weakest position, weaker even than that of non-professional occupations. The main thing from the point of view of the transition theory of stratification is that managerial position has a major impact on incomes among professionals.

The growth of professionalism is an important aspect of post-socialist transition. Describing the situation in Czechoslovakia, Machonin and Tucek (2000, 28) say that:

> it is plausible to think that a part of ruling political, economic and cultural elites as well as the largely non-communist upper-middle occupational and educational strata with inconsistent statuses, were accumulating quite substantial amounts of economic capital, together with important amounts of information (cultural capital) about and contacts (social capital) with the more advanced countries of Western Europe.

Russia differs from the post-socialist countries of Central Europe in the sense that large parts of the working-age population are outside the formal labour market. To cope with the requirements of everyday reproduction and to survive, they need a 'professionalism' of its own kind, i.e. knowledge of networks and contacts. As Simon Clarke (1999, 145) summarizes, 'the density of social networks in which the individual is involved has a very powerful impact on the ability to get a job, to earn more money, to undertake secondary employment and so on.' Clearly then, the rise of professionalism in Russia is still not as significant as in professional society proper.

A high level of education will not alone suffice, but it needs to be complemented by a managerial position. Quite strangely, a managerial position affords high incomes even at the lowest level of education or without a professional position (Tables 15 and 16).

What, then, are the joint effects of a professional position and educational level in managerial positions? We may note that educational level has much greater significance (about four times) among professionals as compared with the group of semi-professionals. It is also clear that the highest educational level is more common in the group of professionals than among semi-professionals.

Table 15
Incomes according to education and managerial position

	Highest educational level	Mean	N
Managerial position	General & unfinished secondary	149	15
	Secondary special & unfinished higher	122	133
	Higher & academic	167	144
	Total	146	292
No authority	Primary	55	25
	General & unfinished secondary	73	235
	Secondary special & unfinished higher	82	502
	Higher & academic	118	184
	Total	86	946
Total	Primary	55	25
	General & unfinished secondary	78	250
	Secondary special & unfinished higher	90	635
	Higher & academic	140	328
	Total	100	1238

What does all this mean for the case of the transition theory of stratification? To me it seems that the effects of professional position and educational resources on incomes both lend support to the theory. However, since the main factor is managerial position, it is clear that the theory needs to be specified.

The results are also understandable in the broader context of Russian transition. The process of privatization in Russia was very much based on old positions and earlier social relations and social capital (Lane 2000). It is also possible that in the group of Russian managers today, there are both old and new actors and that the dividing line runs between public or major old privatized industrial companies and new enterprises of the private sector.

We still need an overall evaluation of the impact of the main explanatory variables on the level of incomes. The joint effect was counted by using different regression models. All the models used gave essentially the same result.

Table 16
Incomes in managerial position by professionalism and education

		Highest educational level	Mean	N
Managerial position	Professionals	Sec special & unfinished higher	98	19
		Higher & academic	176	52
		Total	155	72
	Semi-professionals	Sec special & unfinished higher	87	36
		Higher & academic	110	11
		Total	93	52
	Other	General & unfinished secondary	182	8
		Sec special & unfinished higher	141	77
		Higher & academic	151	79
		Total	148	164
	Total	General & unfinished secondary	147	14
		Sec special & unfinished higher	120	132
		Higher & academic	157	142
		Total	140	288
No authority	Professionals	General & unfinished secondary	21	3
		Sec special & unfinished higher	63	33
		Higher & academic	104	110
		Total	91	157
	Semi-professionals	General & unfinished secondary	63	16
		Sec special & unfinished higher	57	103
		Higher & academic	135	25
		Total	72	144
	Other	Primary	55	25
		General & unfinished secondary	74	216
		Sec special & unfinished higher	91	354
		Higher & academic	142	49
		Total	88	644
	Total	Primary	55	25
		General & unfinished secondary	73	235
		Sec special & unfinished higher	82	501
		Higher & academic	118	184
		Total	86	945
Total	Professionals	General & unfinished secondary	50	4
		Sec special & unfinished higher	74	63
		Higher & academic	127	162
		Total	111	229
	Semi-professionals	General & unfinished secondary	71	21
		Sec special & unfinished higher	65	139
		Higher & academic	128	36
		Total	77	196
	Other	Primary	55	25
		General & unfinished secondary	78	224
		Sec special & unfinished higher	100	431
		Higher & academic	148	128
		Total	100	808
	Total	Primary	55	25
		General & unfinished secondary	77	249
		Sec special & unfinished higher	90	633
		Higher & academic	135	326
		Total	99	1233

Table 17
Beta coefficients in the final model explaining income differences

Education	.12
Gender	.19
Region (1)	–.22
Decision-making position (2)	.16
Pensioner	–.18
Sector: public-private	.11
Unemployed (1)	–.11
Student (1)	–.11

R coefficient for the model was .482 and R square .299. All beta coefficients were highly significant. The regression analysis confirms certain main features of income inequality in Russian society. Both education and a position of decision-making authority are important factors with regard to success. Inequality is also highly dependent on region: people living in the metropolitan region (Moscow, St. Petersburg) are clearly better off than people in rural areas, even though there is greater educational inequality within these areas than elsewhere. The economically non-active groups of the unemployed, students, and pensioners in particular, emerge as the main losers of the transition process. Finally, gender retains its significance among the main explanatory factors of income inequality. All these results are in line with the findings of Commander et al. (1997, 31–2), who additionally showed that successful households have lower dependency ratios (1997, 32).

Reproduction in Underdeveloped Transitional Society

The case of Russian society does not fit in very well with standard theories of modernization (cf. Muller 1992, Strubar 1991 and 1994, and Sztompka 1993). Among the criteria that are not met by the Russian case are as follows:

1) Russia is not a capitalist monetary economy; 2) Its institutions and legislation are not adequate for market and democratic transition; 3) There is in the country a large shadow economy; 4) Wage labour does not provide a sufficient source of income for households and families in the wage earning population, but other income sources are required in what is essentially a subsistence economy; 5) Organized crime plays a major role in the economy; 6) Official social support has remained underdeveloped since the decline of workplace benefits and because of the continuing economic crises.

Russia (and most other CIS countries) has failed to make a successful changeover to market economy. It still lacks the necessary structures and modes of economic regulation. Economic and institutional change has also failed to show any real evolutionary nature (Dunford 1998; see also the contributions by Grabber and Stark, Smith and Swain, who carry further the argument for the importance of institutional regulation).

Dunford (1998, 82) says that in the case of the former Soviet Union, the programme of transition was a complete failure for three reasons:

> first, because the programme involved a false understanding of the nature of communist economies; second, because it failed to anticipate the impact of structural adjustment on an economy that was not already a market economy; and, third, because it was associated with the failure to appreciate the nature of institutions on which capitalism depends and of the mechanisms of (primitive accumulation) involved in the creation of capitalism.

This is an important argument which in essence says that economic failure and the loss of the structural preconditions for normal social reproduction were the result of deliberate policies and a misreading of the situation.

The theory of the success of transitional stratification also does not fit in very well with the case of Russian transformation. As was pointed out earlier, success in the process of transition requires a combination of professionalism and managerial function. In the category of workers, skill qualifications do little to strengthen their position in the labour market. The one exception in this regard is the clear differentiation of incomes according to level of education. However, the effect of education also depends on managerial position, region and age.

The picture changes quite considerably if we take account of the total Russian condition, which must be the context for a conclusive evaluation of everyday reproduction. The starting-point of full employment must first of all be analytically broken down, which represents a challenging task for further research. The material and studies thus far confirm that there is a chain from (labour market and reproduction) positions from the full-time employed to those with no real means of subsistence. Between these extremes there is a whole range of reproduction positions under unstable change. Simon Clarke (1998) concludes:

> In short there is a wide range of statuses in the Russian labour market, with a series of gradations between the small minority who are in regular full time employment, who are paid on time, who earn enough to support themselves at or above the socially established subsistence level and, at the other extreme those who are entirely without employment or any apparent means of subsistence.

One of the current vicious circles in the Russian economy is the lack of money. According to the Russian Economic Barometer in December 1996, barter accounted for 40 per cent of the sales of industrial enterprises. The government itself estimated that almost 70 per cent of all deliveries were exchanged in barter terms (Clarke 1998 and Clarke 1998b). Enterprises have high levels of mutual debts and are unable to secure loans, and to pay their employees' wages on time. The state budget is very limited, and the state does not have the funds for infrastructure investments and for social welfare.

The continuing economic crisis forms the foundation for both the small-scale shadow economy and for large-scale economic corruption and crime.

In the Russian condition all possible social means are needed for reproduction, from plots to relatives and illegal economy. In sum, Russian society remains far removed from a capitalist wage worker society and from the respective reproduction conditions. The need for informal means of reproduction increased with the collapse of workplace services. At the same time this change also had an impact on the conditions for creating social relations and networks and more broadly on workers' solidarity and mobilization (Ashwin 1998).

In an evaluation of the extent of social equality in Russia it is important to take account of the decline in labour market participation, the large-scale poverty and informal sources of reproduction (for example, the significance of plots and social networks). Large numbers of Russian households are currently living well below subsistence levels. According to a study of 4000 households in November 1996, the median household income was 680,000 roubles, and the median income per head was 290,000 roubles. Half of the households earned no more than one-third of the amount they thought they needed to lead a normal life, 83 per cent said they earned two-thirds of this amount and only 7 per cent had what they considered to be enough to live a normal life (Clarke 1998, v-107).

The Russian mode of everyday reproduction is grounded in a negative mixture of elements of an underdeveloped, regionally and socially fragmented non-monetary economy. This explains both the lack and the polarization of reproductive resources – and the unemployment, the non-payment of wages, the lack of social and housing security, and the need to participate in the shadow economy. Nonetheless the picture needs to be complemented with additional elements, which can be clearly seen from the controversy concerning shock therapy (Gowan 1995 and 1996; Lloyd 1996; Dunford 1998). The debate testifies to the importance and influence of Western society, especially the US and the IMF. This foreign influence goes a long way towards explaining the situation of negative stability, the failure to resolve the problems of inequality, polarization and insecurity in everyday reproduction.

Chapter 6

Mental Climate in Russia

Raimo Blom

Theories and Problems

Working within the confines set by the empirical data available and the general theme of our book, this chapter discusses questions related to the mental climate in Russia. The focus is on the aspects of confidence, success factors and conceptions about the future, all of which are relevant to structural conditions and the conditions for everyday reproduction. They should also help to shed light on the differentiation of the mental climate. The analysis also comprises existential beliefs, which assume a somewhat different place: they provide the diffuse general frame for other elements of mental climate. The analysis is grounded in the basic idea according to which mental climate lies in-between the structural conditions and problems of everyday reproduction and the general problem of social integration (see Figure 1).

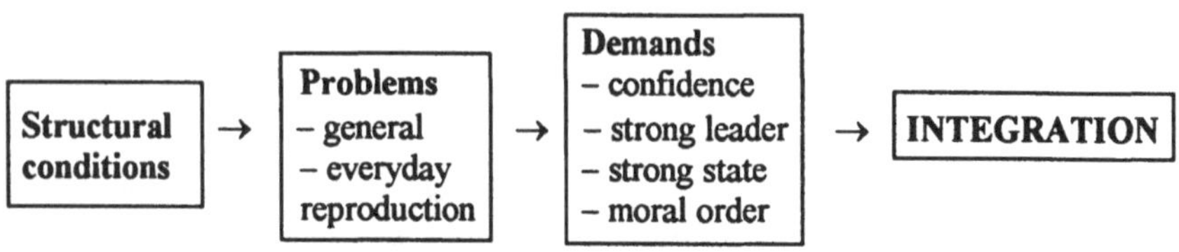

Figure 1
The logical order of things in the analysis of mental climate

The demands listed in the Figure are intended as examples; many other things are expected, such as reorganized production, justice and equality. We shall come back to these issues in the final chapter. Our intention here is to analyse the mental climate in the context of structural conditions and social reproduction. The demands are not drawn from the empirical analysis, but based on interpretations of the empirical measurements of beliefs.

We begin the discussion below with a brief overview of approaches to studying mental climate, which is expected to add more depth to our analysis of the complex theoretical field. In conjunction with the earlier chapters of the book, this discussion should also provide a more solid background to understanding and interpreting the empirical results.

Long and Short History of the Russian Mind

Our efforts to understand the mental climate in Russia are very much complicated by the historical changes that have taken place in Russian and Soviet society. The possibility of radical change and the power of old legacies have both had a constant presence. The structure and culture of Soviet society have been interpreted in many different ways, for instance on the basis of the dichotomies of holy and profane produced by Soviet ideology and social practice (Kivinen 1998), or by reference to the long history of modernization and its structural roots (Aanason 1993). However, we are unable to discuss these interesting analyses here.

The diversity and complexity of the Russian mental climate is clearly in evidence in an examination of the discussion that went on in Russian newspapers in 1995–98. Ideas of an eternal Russia and the special nature of Russian mentality, the long history of Russian autocracy and submission provide examples of the assumed deep layers of the Russian mind. The new situation is in turn clearly reflected in the discussion about new power blocs, groups and clans and about the middle classes (Karppinen 1999).

It was in the course of this discussion that President Yeltsin launched a competition whose purpose was to find the idea of Russia in the new situation. Russia was still thought to be influenced by three cultural heritages, i.e. Byzantine, Tatarian and Western thinking (Grigori Pomerants, Novoje vremja 41/1996, Karppinen 1999, 183). It was also argued that the old Russian way of life was nothing more than a myth, and that life in Russia was a constant economic, ecological and moral crisis. The kind of values that were thought to be needed in Russia were indicative of a western way of thinking, as exemplified by the list of Timofeyev (Izvestija 9 August 1996, see Karppinen 1999, 167ff.): this list included the values of God, fatherland, family and individual success.

Standard theories of modernization do not provide a very convincing account of Russian society (cf. Srubar 1991 and 1994, Muller 1992 and 1996, Sztompka 1993). Therefore a discussion of the type of Soviet/Russian modernization is important for the theory of post-socialist transformation.

The Political Economy of Patience and Social Integration

The integration of post-socialist societies has often been regarded as something of a miracle. Shlapentokh (1995), for instance, has tried to explain the patience of the Russian people at the beginning of transition in 1992–94 which saw a sharp decline and polarization of material wealth yet no reaction on a mass level. Shlapentokh rejects four common theories proposed to explain the absence of a mass response, namely:

- the liberal theory (patience supports reforms)
- the traditionalist theory (patience is a deep-rooted feature of the Russian national character)
- Soviet theory (patience was a product of the Soviet system which instilled obedience to orders from above)
- the elite theory (absence of leaders)

Instead, Shlapentokh (1995, 262–3) says the crucial point was the careful weighing of the prospects of success. On the basis of Russian survey and opinion poll data, Shlapentokh highlights the set of conditions that led to the low evaluation (ibid. 264–75): these included the yearning for social order, stability and physical security, lack of confidence in social programmes, psychological adaptation with time, material adjustment, criminal activity, and alienation from politics and society.

Laszlo Bruszt (1995) takes a broader view than Shlapentokh and asks why people in Russia supported capitalism. He distinguishes between two lines of theoretical argumentation in the explanations offered in post-socialist countries. The first theory, or the so-called incompatibility thesis says that this support is determined by changes in people's structural position and the short-term payoffs that the reforms can deliver. The second theory (deriving from the literature that is described by many authors as the political economy of patience) says that support is not a direct function of changing socio-economic positions, and furthermore that the democratic polity is not merely about representation of people's short-term interests.

Both of these theories need the concept of state. The first regards the autonomous transformative state as necessary, although the autonomy required of the state is undermined by democracy. In the second line of thinking, the democratic state is the prime mediator between the changing economy and lasting support for capitalism. The democratic process itself has plenty of means to influence the level and extent of support. The main thing is the belief in political institutions and in the actors playing a key role in the political process. There are also several other factors that can induce tolerance and patience, such as perceptions of past experience, (low) evaluations of alternative routes, etc.

Bruszt's analysis based on the data from 11 nations seems to lend support to the 'patience thesis'. His empirical analysis also confirms the primary importance of the trust variables in explaining the support of capitalism in Eastern Europe. Underlying different theories are also questions about class and the social differentiation of positions and consciousness. Even though they have no direct influence in terms of legitimising support for social reforms, they certainly have an effect on the space of possible political/democratic manoeuvring. This means that they have an impact on initiatives, on mechanisms of inclusion, feelings of responsibility and on the presentation and evaluation of alternative programmes.

The third line of explanation derives from enterprise level case studies which emphasize the position of worker collectivity in the Soviet Union and changes in that collectivity during the transition period. More on this type of explanation later on in this chapter.

From the 'integration perspective', social integration and system integration are hardly supportive of each other. If social integration focuses on actors and their cooperative or conflictual relationships and system integration on institutions and the compatibility of different structural logics, the time schedules of their changes are very different (Lockwood 1964, Mouzelis 1991; for the concepts of integration, legitimacy and regulation, see Blom 1993).

The best examples of lacking system integration are provided by the underdeveloped economic institutions in Russia. This concerns both contract legislation and the rules of market transaction. The downward logic of real economic development confirms the impossibility of system integration from the economic point of view. The political order has developed in an even more unpredictable way; the rule has been one step forwards and then two or more steps backwards. Moral order has for the main part been absent and also expected in the way our later results will show.

Social integration is necessary from the reproduction point of view. The social network is needed. Nonetheless social integration was based on the division between 'us' and 'them'. Even though this division was made less pronounced during perestroika and the early years of transition, it was heightened again towards the end of Yeltsin's late regime. And judging by the recent incident with the Kursk submarine, it seems that it has become more divisive still.

Difficulties in social integration may arise from two main sources: first, from insufficient experience and knowledge about the systemic change attempted from an 'integration perspective', social integration and system integration are hardly supportive of each other.

Social integration is adversely affected by conflicting pressures. The list is headed by social insecurity, which affects people's everyday interaction, rural poverty and communal disorganization and a generation gap with different life-styles and values. There is a close link between the lack of real interest mediation and problems of social integration. Every society needs channels of interest and communicative mediation in order to have a solid basis for social integration. Social integration also requires a developing sense of justified equality or inequality.

It has also been argued that 'many aspects of the communist era were deeply and often subconsciously internalized by both citizens and officials' (Holmes 1997, 16). These features range from mistrust of political institutions to moral confusion, a widespread sense of insecurity and legitimation problems (Holmes 1997, 16–21).

Many of these problems are common to post-socialist countries. However, Russia is a special case as an earlier leading communist power, as a large country with a special historical experience. There is also evidence that the 'transition culture' as measured by the narratives of Ukrainian and Estonian people is less developed in Russian-type countries than it is in the post-socialist countries of Central Europe. This would suggest that the narratives of transformation are not shaped by the themes of freedom and responsibility to the same extent in Russia as they are in many other post-socialist countries. The common feature of the narratives of Ukrainians and Estonians were region and nation (ethnic themes) and the themes or everyday reproduction (standard of living and employment) (Kennedy 1999, Cpt 4).

Old and New and the Relations of Blat

The mental climate does not derive from the past, but it is a mixture of old and new expectations and experiences in everyday life during transition. We do not have very much faith in the 'long history' or in an 'eternal Russian character'.

The Soviet system produced a special network of informal relations to help people cope in the shortage economy. This network was known as the blat. 'Blat was an exchange of "favours of access" in conditions of shortages and a state system of privileges' (Ledeneva 1998, 37). Importantly, blat was also a moral and cultural foundation.

In her comprehensive study Ledeneva highlights the key difference between blat and other related practices, especially informal relations and the shadow economy. Compared with other related practices, the blat can be viewed as:

> (1) less morally reprehensible and therefore more pervasive than any of these other practices;
> (2) a specific form of social relationship embedded in personal (horizontal, non-hierarchical, compassionate and warm networks);
> (3) a culturally grounded pattern of mentality and behaviour, a form of exchange based upon certain ethical and cultural codes;
> (4) in some ways quite specific to the Soviet system and therefore not amenable to explication apart from such characteristics as perennial shortage and the state system of distribution. (Ledeneva 1998, 52).

It is important to note that blat, as an exchange of 'favours of access', cannot be slotted in the category of either gift or commodity exchange. Instead, it is doubly based on a private relationship and regular communal interaction and also on access to public resources. The debts of honour are diffused and delayed in the case of blat.

In our analysis of mental climate the blat provides the basis for understanding 'the old'. The question is, to what extent and in what way does it still influence the mental climate in Russia in the late 1990s?

The changes taking place in the market are in some respects based on the same basic pillars as the blat. Market exchange and market morals colonize the old 'Lebenswelt'. As we have shown in earlier chapters in this volume, the services that used to be provided through the enterprise level have caved in, which has very much undermined the prospects of exchanging favours in everyday life. The status system at the enterprise level has also changed, though some studies (e.g. Ashwin 1996; Ledeneva 1998, 206–7) have shown that the blatnye (privileged basic workers) are more often better paid than ordinary workers.

The Soviet workplace was a welfare structure in its own right that provided many different welfare services which were important for everyday reproduction. It was also a place of paternalistic domination and collectivism. Collectivism has not lost its significance during the transitional period, but it has been suggested that the relationship to the labour collective has continued to structure workers' behaviour during the changes. That is, the reaction of workers to the pressures of reform has exhibited both an attachment to collective institutions of the past and active development of individual survival strategies. The 'pressures of reform' include problems with wage payment, short time and administrative vacations, redundancies, tightened local labour markets, enterprises' divestiture of *sotkul'tbyt* and the general erosion of social support (Ashwin 1998, 195). Russian patience during the transitional period has also been interpreted from this perspective as a combination of alienated collectivism and individual survival strategies (ibid., 196).

Do we conclude then that the blat is unable to operate in a situation where the non-market ethic and informal relations based on that ethic have disappeared? The answer is (somewhat tentatively) negative. The blat should be able to transform itself according to the changing market conditions, but on the other hand the market conditions in Russia today (as we have seen) are still in many ways deficient. As one expert in commercial law says (Ledeneva 1998, 210), 'it's crucial to remember that banks are not banks, money is not money, and insurance is not insurance'.

The times have really changed. The role of acquaintance, or what in the Soviet period was identical to blat, has very much diminished. Having said that, acquaintance can still help. It can provide information that can help resolve problems; it serves as intermediary in getting introduced to useful persons; it plays an important role in providing informal recommendations; and it plays a major part in the change of power structure from patronage to corruption.

The new Russians of today are more pragmatic than the Russians of Soviet times. They value success, individualism and efficiency; they are professional, decisive, business-like; and they are practical, persistent, even aggressive, and able to cope with difficulties (Kramnik 1995, Ledeneva 1998, 203–4). The new period has been described by Skidelsky (1995, 168; see also Ledeneva 1998, 212) as the end of the 'age of collectivism' and as a lapsing into 'gangster' capitalism, nomenklatura expropriation and rent-seeking.

Our analysis of blat is clearly indicative of change. The process of transformation has not produced an ideal type of modern capitalism or modern democracy, nor have social relations completely changed. There is still need for social support and informal solidarity. The main reason for this lies in the monstrous character of 'new Russian capitalism', which has spelled insecurity and poverty for the vast majority of the population. All this means that the description below of the mental climate in today's Russia must be interpreted within the frame of the struggle between Old and New. The interpretation does not necessarily have very much to do with major questions on the political and ideological arena, and it points more in the direction of difficulties with everyday coping and reproduction rather than an eternal Russian character or the problems of the lost power and honour of Russia.

What, then, are the main dimensions of the mental climate that prevails in Russia today? The analysis below is framed by the general conditions in Russian society discussed earlier: the failure of the national economy during transformation, the highly polarized labour markets and reproduction situations, and weak institutional development, i.e. in short the insecurity of the economic order of non-monetary capitalism and the lack of moral, political and social order. In line with the earlier analysis of the transformation of the blat, we will see that there is a persistent conflict between the old and new way of life, moral code, and the whole order of social relations and their structural foundation. It is also assumed that the homogeneity of the mental limit is a precondition for social cohesion and integration.

Structure of the Mental Climate

The structure of the mental climate in Russia is described on the basis of the main attitude and belief variables from the 1998 survey. The questions concern (1) existential beliefs, (2) confidence in social institutions, (3) factors influencing success in social life, and (4) conceptions of future.

The attitudes and beliefs were factor analysed with the aim of finding some basic (shared) dimensions of the mental climate. We turn now to those dimensions.

Existential Beliefs

The set of beliefs discussed first are those basic orientations in life which are sometimes thought to be the only important things in Russian life. In our analysis they are thought to be the framing dimensions in relation to all other dimensions of mental life. Existential beliefs tend to change more slowly than the other aspects discussed here.

Three preset response options were given to each item: 3 = believe, 2 = believe to some extent and, 1 = do not believe. The factor analysis revealed three main groups of beliefs as follows.

Table 1
Aspects of belief

I Parascientific	II Religious	III Destiny
.72 Extraterrestrial civilizations	.95 Heaven	.57 Signs
.70 Telepathy	.95 Hell	.47 Folk medicine
.70 Astrology	.61 Demonism	.37 Destiny
.66 UFOs	.56 God's punishment for sins	
.61 Extrasensory cure	.31 Second Advent of Christ	

In theory all the items above may be true, but there is not enough evidence to corroborate them. The pattern of beliefs is quite clear in terms of their content. It is interesting to observe that 'international plot against Russia' is included in this same category.

On average one-third of all Russians are believers. On the dimension of religious beliefs, belief in heaven and hell is clearly the strongest factor. Belief in demonism also belongs quite clearly to this dimension. Over one-third of all Russians share these religious beliefs. The highest figure is recorded for God's punishment for sins, with 48 per cent indicating they believe this.

This is a relatively minor factor, explaining only 4 per cent of the variance, while the first factor covers 25 per cent and the second 16 per cent of the variance. It is also a heterogeneous factor in terms of its content. There is very strong belief in the items included in the third factor. Over two-thirds or 68 per cent believe in signs, 85 per cent in popular medicine, and 54 per cent in destiny. Again, the content of this factor is something that may well be true but difficult to establish. Popular medicine is the most practical of the issues covered and also an area on which it is possible to gain some confirmation.

Destiny emerges in this analysis in the top category: people show strong belief in signs, popular medicine and destiny. The difference compared to confidence in political institutions is quite considerable.

Confidence

The second set of variables measured confidence in social and political institutions. The respondents were asked, 'to what extent do you trust' the following institutions (with a five-point response scale). Four factors explained 52.4 per cent of the total variance. The factors were as follows:

Table 2
Aspects of confidence

I Social and political institutions	II Traditional state	III Media	IV Economic power
.82 Council of federations	.84 Courts	.80 Television	59 Banks
.78 State Duma	.73 Police	.79 Newspapers	.56 Entrepre-neurs
.69 Government	.58 Army		
.58 President	.36 Trade unions		
.41 Local authorities	.29 Orthodox Church		

The first factor was a very general confidence dimension, measuring confidence in political institutions and explaining 34.7 per cent of the total variance. The concentration of the variance on this factor is mainly explained by the low confidence shown in politics and its main actors at the time of the survey. On the basis of this evidence the political and social institutions in Russia currently enjoy very limited legitimacy. The combined percentages of 'mainly' or 'fully confident' are: President 3 per cent, Duma 7 per cent, government 16 per cent, courts of justice 16 per cent, and police 15 per cent. The confidence figures for trade unions is 9 per cent, for entrepreneurs 5 per cent, and for banks 3 per cent.

The second dimension gathers the main organs of the state machinery and also trade unions and the Russian Orthodox Church with minor loadings. The clear focus in this dimension is on the institutions of official control and violence. It is interesting that trade unions and the Orthodox Church feature on this dimension, even though the loadings are low. The picture is the same as in Soviet times.

Confidence in the mass media constitutes a dimension of its own. It is indeed important that they do not slot into the same complex as the institutions in general factor or in the earlier dimension of the traditional state. The situation is in fact the same as for example in Finland. Confidence in media institutions is differentiated from confidence in political and state institutions (Blom 1999, 198–9). The fourth factor makes a distinction between political and economic power. Confidence in political and state institutions is not the same thing as trust in banks and entrepreneurs. We must remember that banks are at the very bottom of the confidence scale: only three per cent of the respondents indicate they trust the banks. Although the last two factors do emerge clearly, they do not explain very much of the total variance. The most significant finding was the (low) confidence in political institutions.

Success

One of the key aspects of social life is the question of how to succeed. The spirit of capitalism (or socialism) has long been one of the main issues of social theory. In our survey the conditions for advancing in society were measured using a five-point scale. The questions concerned both today's evaluation and the situation ten years ago (year 1988).

Table 3
Factors of success

I Work and social abilities	II Honesty and law abidance	III Conditions	IV Social connections
.78 Perseverance	.88 Honesty	.61 Foreign contacts	.84 Relatives in managerial position
.66 Hard work	.83 Law abidance	.53 Living in a capital	.72 Rich parents
.55 Natural intellect	.40 Independence	.50 The right nationality	.57 Useful contacts
.54 Ambition	(.36 Appropriate political views)	.36 Luck	
.53 Ability to take risks			
.43 Charm, social qualities			
.39 Good education			

The assessment of the situation in 1998 yielded four main dimensions in factor analysis after Varimax rotation. Four factors explained 45 per cent of the total variance, with the first factor accounting for 24 per cent and the second for 11 per cent.

The first factor combines elements of modern work ethics: perseverance, hard work, ambition, and the ability to take risks, as well as natural intellect, social skills and education. This is the main way in which Russians think one can get ahead in society. Its 'Russianness' lies primarily in the emphasis on capacities and intellect, even personal charm.

The first two items in the second factor constitute the hard core of this view. The last item, 'appropriate political views' is ambiguous in this dimension because it also receives high scores on two other factors (the first and the third). The factor has a clear moral dimension to it: you must be honest and you must have the courage to be independent, you must not be influenced by social coercion or illegal temptations.

In a sense the third factor is all about contacts, which possibly also provide the luck that is needed for success. The factor was named 'Conditions', mainly because the social contacts in the fourth factor have more to do with family relations, while this factor concerns more general conditions. It may be noted that social origin ('the right nationality') is loaded here. The dimension also has an urban and even cosmopolitan flavour to it, with 'foreign contacts' getting the highest factor loading. The fourth factor links social origin and family together with other social contacts. It is a relative dimension of the third factor.

In an attempt to monitor changes in the mental climate, we also inquired about the importance of the same factors to getting ahead in society ten years ago. The results reveal a clear pattern of transition. Factors related to success in the new conditions of capitalist market society have clearly gained in importance compared with the situation in 1988. Family connections, rich parents and relatives in managerial positions are all important. The same goes for foreign contacts, which have assumed more importance than any other factor during the transition, and the ability to take risks. The growing importance of the right nationality and living in the capital region are both part of the same pattern.

The picture becomes clearer still when we observe that hard work and education have lost much of their importance. Honesty and law abidance do not rank among factors of success, but together with appropriate political views they have lost most of their significance.

At the end of 1998 the most important success factors are useful contacts, rich parents and relatives in managerial positions: over 90 per cent of the respondents identify these three conditions as important for success. They are followed by luck (84%) and the ability to take risks (80%). At the other end of the scale we find honesty (37%) and law abidance (33%).

Table 4
Factors influencing success in 1988 and 1998 (important %)

	1988	1998	Difference
Rich parents	54	93	+39
Relatives in managerial positions	69	92	+23
Good education	86	73	−13
Useful contacts	78	95	+17
Hard work	85	67	−18
Perseverance	82	77	−5
Ability to take risks	47	80	+33
Ambition	63	67	+4
Natural intellect	86	75	−11
Living in the capital region	34	54	+20
The right nationality	18	37	+19
Foreign contacts	19	68	+49
Charm, social qualities	65	72	+7
Appropriate political views	65	33	−32
Honesty	71	37	−34
Law abidance	72	33	−39
Independence	44	56	+12
Luck	73	84	+11

On the basis of the picture emerging from the discussion above, what kind of society are we talking about here? Quite clearly, this is a case of capitalism, but with important additional features. This is capitalism without the elements of moral and law; it is capitalism before capitalism. The mental climate and the institutional conditions of market capitalism are still lacking. The ability to take risks is more important now than hard work. Expressions such as 'bribe capitalism' are not too wide off the mark in this connection.

Conceptions of the Future

People's view of the future and the importance of different directions for the future must be examined in relation to the structural changes that have taken place during the transformation period. The background is provided by an underdeveloped, insecure society that has suffered major economic and social losses. Collected shortly after the economic crash of autumn 1998, the answers are indicative of high expectations for the future. They tell us most directly about aspects that are most important for the cohesion and integration of Russian society.

The respondents were presented with the following question: 'There is an ongoing discussion about the preferred directions of development in our society. To what extent are the directions listed important to you personally?'

There were a total of 23 items, with preset responses given on a five-point scale. The respondents were also presented with a card listing the items to make the task of answering easier. The factors were as follows:

Table 5
Preconditions for future success

I Moral	II Production	III Market and democracy	IV Russia
.47 Full employment	.73 Restoration of production	.69 Development of democracy and citizens' initiative	.46 Protecting the rights of ethnic Russians
.55 Struggle against crime	.79 Restoration of agriculture	.82 Development of market economy	.63 Material equality of citizens
.67 Social support for the underdog		.48 Privatization of state enterprises	.46 Unification of former Soviet republics
.56 Provision for individual rights		.65 Full entry into a world economic system	
.52 Containing bureaucracy			
.50 Protecting family and birth rate			
.48 Struggle against alcoholism and drug addiction			
.47 Struggle against corruption			

The first factor is a general dimension which combines material needs, individual rights and the struggle against social corruption. The uniting principle is that of moral concern. It is possible to put an end to the disorganization of society and its various social evils and ultimately to build a better society for the future. Overall this factor draws our attention to the broad range of difficulties experienced in the development of Russian society.

The second factor highlights the state of ruin in which Russian production currently finds itself and the necessity to reorganize production at the centre of development visions.

Third factor comprises demands for a modern state and market, and comes after the demands for moral integration and the restoration of production. The situation is the same as in the Baltic countries in the mid-90s, where people placed basic needs ahead of the modern market society (Blom 1998). This order clearly highlights the importance of problems in everyday reproduction and security to the mental climate.

The last factor combines the equalization of living conditions with regional restoration of Soviet society; in a sense it represents the restoration of Soviet Russia. The demand for material equality clearly testifies to this. The content of the factor comes very close to one of the main topics of the discussion in Russian newspapers. It is also one of the cornerstones of President Putin's foreign policy.

The factors themselves point at the main problems with regard to the future social cohesion of Russian society. The first requirement for a better future is moral integration: it is necessary to get rid of corruption, bureaucracy, alcoholism and drugs and to establish the rights of individuals, particularly those who are less privileged. This is followed by the problems of capitalist market society and the preservation of Russia.

Social Differentiation of the Mental Climate

The mental climate can be either highly homogeneous or strictly differentiated along the lines of the main social categories. The differentiation of the mental climate is historically determined. Russian society today is a transitional one where there is a mixture of both old and new and where new values and aims are also shaped and influenced by earlier socialist ideals. A good example is provided by the blat that was discussed earlier.

Public opinion can change very rapidly. This is seen for instance in the confidence shown in the President, and to a lesser extent in other political institutions. Putin's regime has quickly restored public confidence in political values.

To what extent then is the mental climate in Russia today differentiated in the light of our empirical data, and what are the main lines of social differentiation?

The following variables were included in the final regression analysis: age, region (urban – rural), education (highest level of education), occupation (from non-professional to professional occupations), class (Wright 1997), income (monthly income in roubles), and three dummy variables describing different positions of the economically non-active population (pensioners, unemployed and students).

Occupational position and class location were converted into quasi-quantitative variables. Occupational status was given three values, class position five values from low to high.

In general the level of explanations was significant but relatively low. The level of explanation also varies according to the dimension of mental climate concerned. The multiple correlation R is over or near .20 in four cases: 'confidence in traditional state', 'confidence in institutions of economic power', 'moral and social concern', and 'market and democracy' as important future concerns. In these cases then, there is a sharper differentiation of mental climate than in others.

All other beliefs and attitudes are relatively well shared. The level of differentiation is lowest in success factors and in existential beliefs.

How exactly is the mental climate differentiated, i.e. can we identify common factors of differentiation or does it follow certain dimensions? The mental climate is differentiated first of all along generational lines, then by region (urban – rural) and social position (education, incomes, occupation and class). Taken together, generation and region are more important factors than social position.

Generation (age) has most weight in explaining confidence in political and traditional state institutions and confidence in institutions of economic power. Younger people show more confidence in political institutions and institutions of social power, older people in traditional state institutions. Age is also an important factor in terms of viewing hard work and social skills, conditions and social contacts as important for getting ahead in society: young people believe these are important more often than older people do. Finally, age is also important in beliefs concerning the future. A modern market and democracy are important for the younger generation, moral concern and the restoration of production for older people.

Table 6
Social background and conceptions of development (correlations)

	Moral	Production	Market and democracy	Russia
Gender	.028	–.029	–.014	.066**
Age	.123**	.087**	–.204**	.216**
Rural	.167**	.097**	.028	.232**
Education	–.007	.003	.176**	–.219**
Individual income (roubles)	–.098**	.001	.114**	–.217**
Family income (roubles)	–.132**	–.031	.102**	–.233**
Income level	–.068**	–.012	.190**	–.227**

**Correlation is significant at the 0.01 level (2-tailed).

We can detect a general factor behind the impact of generation, which comes close to the dimension of traditional-modern. Younger people are for modern political and social institutions, and they see the future as lying in the development of a modern market and democracy. The older generation have more confidence in traditional state institutions, and moral and economic restoration is more important for them than the development of markets and democracy.

Region often works in the same direction as age. The best examples here are the belief in traditional state institutions and moral concern in future conceptions. Both these views are held more often by rural than by urban dwellers, though only in relative terms: the mental climate does not differ directly according to the size of the region.

The mental climate is also impacted by social position, which in some (rare) cases is the strongest factor. The exception here is represented by existential beliefs, on which education has the greatest influence: those with a higher education show less belief in parascientific, religious and destiny dimensions.

A closer look at the beta-coefficients in the regression models draws our attention to some interesting points. Indicators of social position have some bearing on people's confidence in political institutions. Region is somewhat more important than age in explaining confidence in the traditional state. Confidence in the mass media shows the lowest total explanatory power in all models. The highest (positive) coefficient is recorded for the dummy variable 'pensioner'. Positive betas are also recorded for income and 'being a student'.

Confidence in institutions of economic power yields a pattern of explanation where younger age, low class but high incomes are associated.

Views about success factors were widely shared. The most important distinguishing factor here was generation, with younger people viewing hard work and social skills, good conditions and good family and social contacts as more important than older people. The importance of region appears here in two cases: people from rural areas show stronger belief in honesty and law abidance as a source of success, while urban dwellers attach more importance to social contacts. Low social position shows a weak association to regarding honesty and law abidance as a source of success.

All existential beliefs are associated with a low level of education. This is most clearly seen in the case of parascientific and religious beliefs. A low position in the occupational hierarchy and in case of parascientific beliefs and belief in destiny have some effect.

Moral and social concerns and the importance of developing modern markets and democracy show the highest explanatory power. Moral concern is mostly associated with living in rural regions, but also with a low level of education and indicators of low social position. In the economically non-active population pensioners and the unemployed underline the importance of moral concern, the students are against it. The emphasis on modern market and democracy is more typical in younger generations, and is interestingly associated with low class and low education and high incomes. The importance of restoring production and preserving Russia are widely shared future values. Both are associated with living in rural areas and older age. The importance of preserving Russia is also associated with indicators of a low social position.

In sum then, we may say that the mental climate in Russia is relatively homogeneous. On the other hand it does seem to change quite rapidly, at least as far as dimensions of confidence are concerned. It is also divided, mainly along the lines of generation and region and to some extent along lines of social position.

The mental climate in Russia today clearly combines elements of both the old and new. Older people and rural dwellers show confidence in the traditional state and are suspicious of banks and other institutions of economic power. They also emphasise the importance of solving social problems and raising moral concerns together with the revival of production. The younger generation and urban dwellers have faith in political institutions, in hard work, social skills and new social contacts as success factors, and they also emphasize the key importance of modern market society and democracy for the future development of Russia.

Overall the picture is indeed clearly a combination of old and new elements in the mental climate: the traditional state as opposed to new political institutions, markets and financial powers as opposed to moral and social concern. The support for new is typical of the younger generation and urban dwellers, and there is some indication that this has to do with incomes, not with education or profession. Old people, rural dwellers and often people in lower positions are worst off, and they would therefore like to see the old mentality and its concern for justice preserved, no matter how biased it was in practice.

Broken Community

Russian society is in a state of misery. It is also highly polarized both in terms of reproduction situations and welfare and in terms of social power and influence. There is, on the one hand, a small economic elite of the nouveaux riches, on the other hand the vast majority of the population live below the poverty line. There is no real connection between the elite and the people. This is reflected in the low confidence shown towards political and economic institutions and in feelings of socio-political alienation and apathy.

Our empirical analysis draws attention to organizing frames of the mental climate, highlighting the main dimensions of attitudes, orientations and beliefs. The structure of the mental climate is described in important but a limited number of themes: confidence, resources and conditions for success, existential beliefs and conceptions about the future.

The transformation of the mental climate in Russia has not been taking place in isolation from structural changes or changes in reproduction conditions. As was described in Figure 1, we need to move our analysis from structural conditions and from reproduction conditions to the mental climate and in this way to try and gain a deeper understanding of the problems of social integration in Russia.

Conditions here refer primarily to the economic, political and socio-moral institutional and structural situation in Russia. Closely related to these conditions are social problems such as crime, corruption, general insecurity, the absence of social rules and problems of everyday reproduction (low incomes and the lack of housing, health and social services). Demands, then, are indicative of the experiences and the understanding of one's situation in relation to the broader structural and institutional context. The importance of getting production and agriculture back on track points very much in the same direction.

'Crony capitalism' plays a major part in securing the economic rents of a limited number of oligarchs and at once lies behind the current polarization and reproduction problems. The economic rents are derived from the export of raw materials (fuels, metals) and appropriated by global trading corporations and their Russian allies. Tax revenue represents the other main source of economic rent. As a cost of funding the budget deficit, it is appropriated by commercial banks and their international partners (Clarke 2000). The reproduction problems are 'derived' from this appropriation and the related underdevelopment of a large part of production and services.

The mental climate in Russia must be seen in the light of the everyday problems of reproduction and the spectacles taking place in the public space. Because of this mixture public opinion changes in some respects very quickly; an example is provided by confidence in institutions and socio-political actors.

At the time of the survey the figures for public confidence were at a very low level. No more than four per cent indicated they had trusted the President. Today, President Putin enjoys the confidence of over 70 per cent of the population. The survey results are also indicative of high expectations for strong leaders and for reviving production. Somewhere in the picture is the national self-respect of Russians. Perhaps Putin is the authoritarian answer to these demands.

The main future expectation is for moral order. The following items were identified by 90 per cent of the respondents as important future issues: 'campaign against the crime', 'preventing the disintegration of the country', 'fighting against corruption', 'full employment', 'social support for the poor' and 'securing individual rights'. In the light of these opinions social coping and moral reform go very much hand in hand. In people's minds crime and corruption were seen as the main reasons for poverty and social problems, and indeed there is evidence that this comes quite close to the truth of Russian transition.

This analysis is confirmed by the empirical material collected for our survey. According to our respondents the 'appropriation of profits by the few' (87%) and 'poor reform management' (85%) are the main reasons of poverty.

The conditions for success had changed during the past ten years. Useful contacts and rich parents are necessary, honesty and law abidance less so. This is in line with the result according to which 70 per cent of the respondents (fully or mainly) agree with the statement, 'A few strong leaders can do more than the law'.

The interpretation suggested here is that the Russian mental climate today closely corresponds to the underdeveloped nature of the process of transition in Russia and to the huge problems of everyday life it has caused. The mental climate reflects a very marked difference between hopes and reality. Future hopes and expectations are not completely in line with the receipts of success. Morals are seen as important for the future, but in Russian society today it is best to forget honesty and law. The ideal society and everyday reality are far removed from each other.

Putin's regime holds out a promise of law and order. At the same time, however, it has been investing more and more budget resources into defence. Also, there have been signs of an increasing concentration of powers in the Kremlin, even though no changes have been made to the constitution. The long-term reform programme also offers promises of material welfare as part of the new social contract. The state will help the poor, while the oligarchs will be guided towards economic development, job creation and stability. The 'lure of authoritarian temptation' (Sutela 2000) lies at the heart of Putin's programme. Whether it can turn into something else will remain to be seen.

Chapter 7

Values in Contemporary Russian Society

Michail Chernish

The debate on the impact of values on the transition period in Russia has continued to gather momentum ever since the reforms were set in motion by Mikhail Gorbachev. In the late 1960s the debate focused on the Soviet period and the possible impact of values on the becoming of totalitarian society. It was often argued that the specific Russian values were conducive to the communal values of socialist society and concomitant life practices. The philosopher A. Tsipko maintained that the victory of Stalinism was based on the 'military barrack' psychology characteristic of the Russian population, a psychology described early by Karl Marx (Tsipko 1988). These attitudes contributed to a deformation of the original ideas of the Russian revolution and brought about Stalinist terror. A similar approach was raised by Markku Kivinen (2000), who insisted that the process of reform was directly influenced by the unchanging character of Russian values. Russian culture and its deeply embedded traditions, he argues, are determining the Russian path and preventing it from making the best possible use of the market system. Contemporary Russian historian E. Soloviev (1990) takes a different angle, maintaining that the war and other cataclysms of Russian life uprooted millions of peasants and fostered 'legal nihilism' that left an indelible imprint on the Russian mind by changing the Russian language. Another contemporary historian (Ahiezer 1991, 1997) describes the Russian past and present in terms of cultural value cycles: each of which carries a certain set of basic values that determine the shape of society. The basic values of Russian life are *vechevaia* (collective direct democracy) and *authoritarian*. In the twentieth century both of these basic values had to accommodate another basic attitude – the *utilitarian* one. As a result the space between the extremes to which Russian culture is so inclined is gradually being reduced – a process that promises positive change in Russian society.

While critical of the Russian mind of the past, most Russian and some foreign researchers of the perestroika period remained fairly optimistic about the future. Russian history of the twentieth century was viewed as a great cultural experience that would facilitate passage to a new, fair market system and, as Mikhail Gorbachev stated, lead to the construction of a law-based society. However, as it became clear that the reforms were not going according to plan and the visions of a bright future were increasingly dimmed by mounting problems, the debate on values resumed with renewed force and with fewer optimistic overtones. The Russian crisis played into the hands of 'cultural' analysts who insisted that Russian values carried numerous flaws that undermined the rational policies and made it impossible to create anything but 'crony' capitalism. These arguments were summarized in an interview given to a western paper by one of the architects of Russian privatization policy, A. Koch. Koch argued that the failure of many of the reforms was not in fact due to the misguided policies, but to the failure of the Russian people to assimilate the right values and to engage in constructive market-oriented activities. It was hardly surprising that Koch wanted to rid himself of all responsibility for the creation of corrupt 'crony' capitalism. By talking to a western paper, he counted on a friendly ear from western politicians and social scientists, many of whom had long entertained serious doubts about the ability of the Russian population to make a quick and successful transition to the market. However, whatever the content of the message, it raised major questions about whether Russian society was homogeneous in its values and whether the Russian elites and the population at large shared the same basic attitudes.

The ongoing debate highlighted the following fundamental issues related to the values of the Russian population: What are the Russian values? Are they hostile to the market, private property? Are they different from western values and if so, how? Are they immutable values, propped up by a thousand years of Russian history, or are they influenced by structural change and/or cultural development? How homogeneous is Russian society in terms of its values? Are there any basic values that are shared by the entire population, or are there different sets of values that have very little in common?

The data available from the SDMR study allow us to make a contribution to the debate and draw some tentative conclusions. The study was concerned with a limited scope of basic issues such as poverty and its causes, freedom and human rights, justice, law, the state, attitudes towards the educated class. All of these issues were formulated in attitude statements, and the respondents were asked to indicate how far they agreed or disagreed on a five-point scale.

Origin of Poverty

Poverty is a fairly new phenomenon in Russia. In the Soviet era there were large numbers of people who could barely make ends meet. However, they could hardly regard themselves as poor because a) there was an extensive state programme of social assistance, and b) the gap between the rich and the poor was not so great, and the poor did not feel uncomfortably different from any particular privileged group. If there was such a difference, it could easily be attributed to the injustice of the system or to an unfortunate cluster of circumstances. Now that shop windows in major Russian cities are full of goods and foreign luxury cars on the streets indicate the presence of a more successful stratum, Russian citizens face the task of elaborating a more or less coherent explanation as to why they have not grasped the opportunities of the new economic conditions. There are several possible ways to do so. One strategy (the 'social' one) consists in blaming the injustice of the system that favours a few privileged oligarchs. Another explanation puts the blame on the past system that 'depraved' the population by not creating incentives for productive labour. A third strategy might put the blame on the lack of individual excellence such as education or intellect, and a fourth on general bad management of the reform process.

It is clear from the responses that the social approach is favoured most.

Table 1
Causes of poverty (mean on a five-point scale)

	Means	SD
Poverty is caused by the fact that profits go to a handful of oligarchs	4.53	0.82
Poverty is caused by bad management of the reform process	4.54	0.82
Poverty is caused by the fact that some people simply do not want to work	2.89	1.54
Poverty is caused by the fact that some people lack the intellect	2.77	1.44

Table 2
Principle component analysis (unrotated, factor scores)

	Component	
	1	2
Poverty is caused by the fact that some people lack the intellect	.859	–.156
Poverty is caused by the fact that some people simply do not want to work	.859	–.153
Poverty is caused by the fact that profits go to a handful of oligarchs	.189	.775
Poverty is caused by bad management of the reform process	.153	.785

There is clearly a strong belief in society that the main cause of poverty is a) the greed of the oligarchs who appropriate all public wealth and b) incompetent managers who are in charge of the reform process – an obvious invective in the direction of former president Yeltsin and a succession of reformist Prime Ministers. We conducted a factor analysis on the basis of the above questions.

As we can see assessments of the cause of poverty are neatly divided into two distinct patterns. The first, somewhat weightier pattern than the second (explaining 38 and 31% of the variance, respectively), lays the blame on the Russian elites, their greed and lack of management skills. The second is the direct antithesis to the former. It attributes the cause of poverty to the qualities of the people, their lack of intellect and laziness. The strength of the first factor was quite predictable in view of the results of the primary analysis, the strength of the second one requires closer analysis before we can draw any conclusions with respect to what it represents. Further analysis led us to select those respondents who were determined that popular degradation caused poverty rather than the lack of integrity on the part of the elites. We chose those who attributed the rank of four or higher to the statements blaming the people, and the rank of three or lower to the statements blaming the elites. It turned out that such a set of attitudes was characteristic of a minuscule number of people, just 0.5 per cent of the population. Predictably these were fairly well-to-do (53% of those who either have no problems or have money problems only when they have to make a major purchase such as a house or an apartment) respondents employed in the private sector. A much bigger part (15.4%) of the population shared both value sets. The breakdown into income groups showed that this category was no different from the rest of the population: the proportions of the rich, the middle stratum and the poor were very similar. The data available allow us to conclude that the Russian population upholds three basic stereotypes of poverty causes: 'blaming the elites', 'blaming the people' and 'blaming both'. Only the highest elite stratum is prepared to exonerate itself from all responsibility for the widespread poverty, the overall majority thinks differently and is either prepared to share responsibility or places it squarely on the rich and the powerful.

Just Society

The more sharply Russian society is divided into the rich and the poor, the more the issue of social justice becomes relevant in the public discussion on past events and the future. What does a just society mean in the eyes of the Russian population? Is it a socialist society where people are equal in terms of wealth? Can education and skills be the basis of difference? Should a just society carry responsibility for providing each citizen providing with free education or medical care, or is it a society where all citizens are on their own? These were the questions that were presented to the respondents of the SMDR study. The following Table described the main results:

Table 3
Conceptions of the features of a just society (mean on a five-point scale)

	Means	SD
In a just society all people enjoy the same standard of living	3.01	1.51
In a just society hard-working people live better	4.48	0.88
In a just society educated people live better	4.13	1.13
In a just society each citizen has the right to free education and medical care	4.58	0.82

The first 'egalitarian' attitude statement gets a rather lukewarm reception, all other statements enjoy broader approval. Just society is seen as one where work and skills account for the difference in wealth and free education and medical care are available to all citizens. In other words, a just society is regarded as a fully meritocratic social arrangement where achievement in work or excellence in education may be conducive to material prosperity and where the state takes care of people's basic needs. There is a temptation to qualify this set of views as a social democratic one, but for one detail that has been omitted from the statistical analysis: this concerns the meaning of the corps terminology employed in the statement. For instance, later projects have shown that there is considerable variation in the population in terms of how they define the term 'work'. An in-depth interview project by a team from the Institute of Sociology revealed that the most widespread understanding of work only comprises those activities that lead to the growth of public wealth. The occupation of a broker or deputy of the State Duma, for instance, are not viewed as that kind of activity, but are judged as forms of a self-seeking redistributive pastime that is detrimental rather than beneficial for society as a whole. The egalitarian idea that was so strong in the past was undermined by the process of reforms and the reality of differentiation, the idea of growth and development remained and became even stronger in the period of prolonged crisis and rising unemployment.

Freedom or Wealth and Stability?

We included in our list two mutually contradictory statements, one claiming that freedom is a greater value than superpower status, the other qualifying stability and higher living standards as more important values than either freedom or human rights.

Table 4
Valuation of freedom and wealth (mean on a five-point scale)

	Means	SD
Stability and higher living standards are more important than freedom or human rights	3.26	1.39
Freedom is a greater value than superpower status	3.26	1.34

It was hypothesized that these statements would run in opposite directions and lead to the identification of two groups with distinct profiles: 'freedom lover' and 'freedom haters'. However, the data clearly proved this hypothesis wrong. It turned out that there was no tangible association: the Pearson correlation coefficient equal to only –0.065 was below significance level. The lack of cohesion in the public mind pointed at a public schism in the understanding of what the ultimate goal of Russian society should be. The basic question is posed as follows: should Russia continue to seek the status of superpower or/and should it concentrate primarily on trying to uphold the living standards of the people? In both cases, freedom is regarded not as an ultimate goal but as an instrumental value that can be a bargain in a trade-off leading to prosperity or/and superpower status. The true 'freedom lovers' defined as those who value freedom beyond prosperity (equal or less than 2 on the first statement) and superpower status (equal or more than 4 on the second one) account for 12.5 per cent of all respondents – a significant part of the population but still numerically less than the majority that treats freedom as a hostage value to other, more traditional aspirations. The 'freedom-haters' or respondents who chose a reverse set of values accounted for an even smaller proportion, or 11.2 per cent. The majority placed themselves in-between the two groups, pointing to a flexible trade-off-oriented set of attitudes.

Power and Law

The study included several attitude statements relating to the mentioned issues: a statement indicating an authoritarian attitude ('A few strong leaders can do more for the country than laws and talk'), a statement stressing the importance of the popular influence ('All people should have the right to influence the policy of authorities'), a statement favouring education ('The management of the country should be in the hands of experienced, qualified people'), a statement emphasizing the dominance of law ('Every citizen must abide by the law'), and a statement underlining the instrumental treatment of law ('It is hard to survive now without breaking the law').

Table 5
Attitude to power and law (mean on a five-point scale)

	Means	SD
All citizens must have the right to influence politics	3.85	1.23
The management of the country should be in the hands of qualified people	4.82	0.48
Some strong leaders may do more for the country than laws and talk	4.06	1.30
Every citizen should abide by the law	4.57	0.79
It is hard to survive now without breaking the law	3.53	1.40

There is a fair amount of agreement with all the above statements, despite their contradictory character. There is an obvious desire to shift the brunt of decision-making to 'qualified and experienced leaders', and at the same time there is general support for the statement that not only the 'qualified and experienced' should lead the nation, but also every citizen should be able to exert some influence. The two statements about the law provide another example of inherent contradictions. The idea of a life based on law receives overwhelming approval from all quarters, and at the same time there is an above average endorsement of the statement calling for a tolerant attitude to breaking the law. On the basis of the above data it might be conjectured that the general contradiction could be explained by the breakdown of the population into distinct groups. A hypothesis may be formulated stating that value integrity resides within groups rather than in the consciousness of the population as a whole. To test this hypothesis, we resorted again to principal component analysis.

Table 6
Principal component analysis (rotated Varimax solution)

	Component	
	1	2
It is hard to survive now without breaking the law	0.0	.735
Every citizen must abide by the law	.752	–.313
All people must have equal chances to influence the policy of authorities	.656	.176
The management of the country should be in the hands of experienced, qualified people	.562	.263
A few strong leaders can do more for the country than laws and talk	.198	.644

The factor analysis produced two major factors accounting for 50 per cent of the variance. In the first, 'heavier' factor (explaining 28%) the emphasis was on two values, i.e. law abidance and popular influence on public policies. The idea of delegating certain powers to qualified managers emerged with a weaker, though significant loading. The second factor stressed an opposite set of values, i.e. a situational attitude to law and an emphasis on authority. The first type may be described as the mainstay of positive change, the supporter of institution creation, the second as a personality type looking for an opportunity beyond stable institutions in the murky waters of criminal marginality and in the individual powers of an authoritarian leader. In the parlance of Marxian analysis, this is the lumpen proletariat, a group consisting of individuals without stable ties with societal structures, degraded and unprincipled. The strength of this factor is further proof of the crisis in the reform process that led to impoverishment and job loss for millions of Russian citizens, thus creating fertile soil for the consolidation of the lumpen proletariat type of consciousness.

Overall Value Typology

Finally, we proceeded to summarize our data on the basis of principal component analysis. It was hypothesized that basic attitudes towards freedom, the state and the law and justice are interlinked and constitute distinct personality types.

The analysis rendered a matrix containing six distinct components. We suppressed the values below 0.2 to make the profile of each component more distinct. The first three components account for roughly the same proportion of the variance (just over 10%), the fourth and fifth cover over 8 per cent and the last one 7.6 per cent.

The first component clearly places the emphasis on three major statements. The strongest belief here is that poverty is caused by the lack of intellect and lack of desire to work on the part of the people. There is also a moderate association with the idea of total independence and self-reliance. An appropriate name for this type of mentality would be 'elitist'. An attempt to link the factor with basic demographic variables did not reveal any spectacular profiles. The factor is slightly younger than the population as a whole, but this seems to be all that distinguishes it from the rest of the population.

Table 7
Factor analysis matrix (Varimax rotated)

	Component					
	1	2	3	4	5	6
Poverty caused by lack of intellect	.859					
Poverty caused by lack of desire to work	.847					
Poverty caused by the misappropriation of public wealth		.438	.308	.208	-.352	
Poverty caused by bad management of Reform		.224	.540		-.262	
Stability and higher living standards are more important than freedom				.709		
It is possible to resign from superpower status for freedom					.747	
In a just society all have an equal standard of living		.252		.617	.273	
In a just society hard working people live better			.718			
In a just society educated people live better			.746			
In a just society each has the right to free medical care and education		.504	.202	.331		
Each should be on his or her own	.330	-.232		.219	.511	
It is hard to survive now without breaking the law			.233	.308	.251	.440
Each citizen must abide by the law		.667				
All citizens must have the right to influence policies		.650				.232
The country's management should be in the hands of experienced people		.279		-.272		.653
A few strong leaders may do more for their country than laws						.692

The second component is prepared to emphasize the importance of many more values. It displays three levels of attachment to various values emphasized by the factor scores. The strongest emphasis is placed on the ability of ordinary citizens to influence public policies and the obligation of each citizen to abide by the law. Both of these are positioned in this type of thinking as inter-related: the elites running out of control, violating the law and pursuing policies against the interests of the people are clearly a cause of concern for this type. Apart from a pro-democracy stance, it embraces the view that every citizen should have access to free medical care and education and that poverty is misappropriated by a handful of oligarchs. In other words, all of these accents fall into a coherent line of reasoning: currently the elites are out of public reach, it allows them to appropriate and redistribute wealth and as a result the rights of citizens are violated, the right to medical care and education is jettisoned. A fairer deal may be struck only if every citizen does his or her bit to influence public policies. This type may be defined as the 'pro-democracy type'. The correlation of the factor with demography variables again did not yield any particular patterns.

The third component brings to the fore two major values: hard work and education. Bad management of the reform process is blamed for the country's current troubles. This type places emphasis on hard work and education – traditional middle class values shared by many of the old Soviet middle class that regarded themselves as a party to an unwritten deal with the state amounting to the following: we do our duty, work hard and put our skills to the service of the country. In exchange we hope for a fair amount of social care. Neither democracy nor freedom was part of the deal. The type can be qualified as the 'old middle class'. The correlation with demographic variables further confirms the conclusion that the factor is closely linked with education. The higher the education of the respondent, the more he or she is likely to share the above system of values.

The fourth type stresses the necessity to sacrifice freedom for higher living standards and calls for a society in which all citizens would enjoy approximately the same standard of living. It also emphasizes the right of citizens to have free medical care and access to education. It puts moderate, though tangible accent upon the idea that survival without resorting to crime is close to impossible in contemporary Russian society. The latter statement is more of an accusatory stance that a line of action. The egalitarian calling for reduced freedom would hardly be in a position to undertake illegal activity. A specificity of this type is that while calling for reduced freedom, it does not favour arbitrary rule by a dictator, nor does it put more emphasis on law and order. Stability is its keyword, and freedom is just a pawn in a trade-off that it is prepared to sacrifice if that is required by the coveted ideal. Further analysis reveals that this factor tends to be correlated with education, employment status and general satisfaction with living standards. In other words, the factor's system of values tends to receive support from less educated respondents, from the unemployed and those who are dissatisfied with their living standards.

The fifth type embraces the liberal viewpoint. It singles out two major values: the idea that superpower status should be abandoned to preserve freedom and that each individual in society is on his or her own. It puts moderate accent on the fact that in the current situation wealth is appropriated by the few. In an even more moderate way, it draws attention to the idea of justice in the form of equality of all citizens. The latent logic underlying this type of reasoning runs as follows: there is a trade-off between superpower status and a better running of the country. The fact that the elites pursue the lost ideal of greatness creates ample opportunity for bureaucracy to commit more resources to superpower projects, leaving citizens to solve their problems on their own. The respondents supporting this value set are slightly richer and younger than the population as a whole. The younger, as has been confirmed by previous studies, tend to put less emphasis on superpower status than the older generation accustomed to Soviet grandeur.

The last type resembles one that has already made itself obvious in the above analysis. It is committed to the idea of an authoritarian leader that can right all the country's wrongs and places accent on the inability to avoid the zone of crime in the current Russian situation. It is again strongly linked with two variables, i.e. employment status and education. The correlations with both are negative, which means that the views expressed by it are likely to get more support from respondents with a lower education and an unstable employment status.

Conclusion

Our analysis above underlines one fact: in a society gripped by crisis, values are often weighed against one another, with some deemed as more important than others. In response to the deformed need structure that stresses survival beyond all other commitments, the values are ranked as 'vital', 'less vital' and 'sacrificable', the latter often being the loftier ones but with less immediate effect on living standards. 'Sacrificable' values may also include 'superpower status' or 'law' depending on the individual's background and his or her current location in the social structure. Hence it is obvious that values cannot be reduced to the legacy of the past. They are a system in a state of flux with different priorities emerging in response to changes in a political and economic situation.

Chapter 8

Restoration of Class Society in Russia?

Jouko Nikula

The question as to whether Russia is witnessing a restoration of class society might seem a rather peculiar one to ask; after all the ongoing process of transition and transformation is in essence about the (re)construction of capitalist society based on social relations, which characteristically are class relations based on private ownership. One can also ask whether there is any point in debating the question as to whether or not a certain country or countries are capitalist, because even Russia clearly meets the most important 'criteria' of capitalist society: there is now private ownership of the means of production and a category of formally free wage labourers. But of course capitalism, even in the most general sense of the term, is about much more than that: there should also be formal detachment of the economy from politics so that economic actors can have no immediate influence on politics. There should also be some institutional forms of civil society, together with specific norms and laws regulating the economy and society. Finally, there should be various institutional and legal arrangements that respond to various needs and problems in the functioning of society, such as social services, educational institutions, banking and insurance institutions, a developed labour market, etc. This is not to say that in order to qualify as capitalist a country should meet all of these criteria: even in the category of countries generally labelled as 'western' there are of course very different kinds of arrangements in place.

As we have seen in the previous chapters of this volume, the Russian version of capitalism only meets a few of these criteria: the Russian economy is not fully detached from politics, the country's institutions and systems of regulation are very deficient, its labour markets are underdeveloped, etc.

Conceptualizations of Russian transition as non-monetary capitalism (Clarke) or as chaotic formation (Lane) highlight related aspects of the 'Russian transition'. Concepts like 'many economies' (Rose) or 'deficient wage-worker society' (Blom) refer to certain aspects of this process. If we add to these the importance of personal networks and new forms of blat as means of survival and getting ahead and the changing conceptions about the conditions for success, we should begin to have the 'Russian transition' in a nutshell. These structural features also provide the basis for an analysis of power, elites and hegemony in Russian society.

The process of transition in Russian society has been full of jumps: the model of transition has been more or less exceptional, and in every case non-linear. Yeltsin's government marked an important turning-point, however: it was during his reign that the government lost much of its ability to control the country's political and economic development. From another angle, this meant there was no turn to the institutional regulation required by the process of transition.

Our analysis highlights many related developments. Russian society today is highly polarized, and poverty is rife. The inequality in everyday life and social reproduction is strictly hierarchic. Many categories of the economically non-active population are at the frontier line of the underclass, and the working population is also hierarchically divided according to income sources, payment or non-payment of wages, economic networks and regions, economic sectors and a range of other factors. Location in the informal economy, in relations of transformed blat and also in the illegal economy are important. For example, one study from 1997 indicated that three-quarters of Russian oil executives and politicians agreed that corruption is widespread, while two-fifths of the oil executives and four-fifths of the politicians thought that Russian economic life in general had a criminal character (Lane 2000, 191).

A growing body of research on Russia and many countries of Eastern and Central Europe clearly demonstrate that even though considerable progress has been made in the creation of the key institutions of market economy, there is still a deep-seated lack of trust in political and economic institutions and a profound sense that organizational failures are common, forcing people to rely on informal social networks to amend these shortcomings. The problems are manifested in: a) widespread anomie; b) social isolation of citizens; c) absence of interest organizations, trade unions and local party activity; d) inefficiency of state institutions and enterprises; and e) corruption, tax evasion and various mafia-type phenomena like bribery. All these very much jeopardize the chances for economic growth and the build-up of confidence in formal institutions such as the party system and democracy in general.

As in many other countries, the early stages of transition in Russia were characterized by 'a period of movement society' when informal movements, interest organizations and other associations mushroomed and organized vast numbers of people. However as soon as the economic reforms got under way and it became clear how badly they were failing, the 'movement society' was replaced by an 'adaptation and survival society', draining organizations and movements from activity and membership. Survey after survey testified to the rapid decline of popular trust in President Yeltsin and his government, which one after the other failed to create and pursue reliable reforms.

Militant worker activists, often without the support of their unions, have already set in motion several waves of protest in Russia. However, despite these occasional outbursts of protest activism, the general level of civil unrest in the country has been astonishingly low. In an attempt to provide a meaningful explanation, commentators have referred to everything from Russian culture and the legacy of communism to the lack of new revolutionary forces. In all these interpretations the subjects have been transformed into objects, a homogenous mass guided from above. However, there is nothing very surprising about the absence of mass-scale social protests in a situation where people have to spend most of their energies sorting out their daily life. With all the chaos that has prevailed, people have simply wanted to see some order and predictability in their lives. Recently there has been much talk about the 'mental characteristics' of Russian people. Within this debate the notion of learned helplessness in 'collective mentality' has gained some support. According to this line of argumentation people are still inclined to think that it is the state's responsibility to provide them with work and social protection. To overcome this 'post-communist syndrome', people have to learn to take responsibility of their own destinies by social political means, by reducing their reliance on subsidies and allowances, etc.

On the surface of it the argument above comes close to the views of Pjotr Sztompka (1993). According to Sztompka the most difficult task in post-socialist transition is the transformation of habits, values and valuations. The root problem lies in the divergence between the fake modernity of socialist society and real, pluralist and democratic modernity. Sztompka argues that the key precondition for real modernity is the development of civilizational competency, which comprises business culture, civic culture, discursive culture and every-day culture.

This theme has subsequently been upgraded into a theory of the role and relations between formal and informal institutions, where formal institutions include banks, laws, and the parliamentary system, while informal institutions comprise values, norms and habits. One aspect of informal institutions is trust, and the key problem in Russia as in other post-socialist countries is that trust is confined to limited circles, whereas at the societal level there is a threat of generalized mistrust.

Raiser (1999) says that the task of increasing trust rests with governments and politics, but there is reason to doubt whether that argument can be valid in a country such as Russia where social and political power is scattered between many rival organizations. In these cases informal network relations or processual trust are very important, providing an opportunity to obtain financial and other resources and therefore representing a clear continuity of network relations that existed during the socialist period. If the preconditions for firms and private persons continue to fluctuate and remain as unpredictable as they have been to date, then there is a real risk of network relations becoming institutionalized and their transforming into a structural element of society. More important than government actions and politics as such is the role of civil society – that people have the means and channels to articulate their problems and interests.

Contemporary Russia is a class society that has seen a dramatic increase in social differentiation during the past 10 years. Hired managers have emerged as winners from the process of transition in that their economic power has clearly increased because of privatization, but the majority of the population has experienced economic and social decline. Only less than one per cent of the population indicated they had no problems with money. Our results suggest that the biggest social class in Russia is represented by the working class, and unskilled workers are the biggest single social category. This clearly testifies to the cruel fact that old qualifications are no longer enough today.

The stratification system among those at work has not changed strictly in line with the transition theory of stratification. Education has assumed clearly greater significance, meaning that reproduction conditions are now differentiated more clearly according to education than at the beginning of transition. Nonetheless it is still necessary to have a managerial or bureaucratic position in order to secure a high economic position.

We have also witnessed the birth of a new elite, commonly described as the 'new Russians'. During the early 1990s the old economic and political elite, the nomenklatura, gained de facto control and partly ownership of the major economic assets. The old elite also constitutes the hard core of the new Russians. It is estimated that about one per cent of the population are members in the new elite: these people are the true winners of transformation.

The elites are not very unified in Russia, but they differ widely in terms of their social origin, social ties, habitus and political attitudes. The transformation of executive capital was the most important asset of the new economic elites, while the earlier party position was not particularly important. What has been important at least for part of the elites are administrative and general cultural capital.

Opinions also vary among the Russian elites on the reforms needed in the country. In many cases the elites are also regional, local and sectoral. They may be socially and organizationally closed, as in the case of the oil elite. Their needs for the support of the state vary widely. Elites may be involved large clans and internal struggles, as in the case of Putin's political regime where the elites have a strong position in terms of mass media ownership.

The Russian transition qualifies many assumptions about the process of transition. In addition to the structural questions mentioned above, we need to point out three things. Professionalism does not have the same significance in Russia as it does in other post-socialist countries with respect to achieving elite positions. Our results on the mental climate in Russia pointed at the differentiation of younger generations from older ones.

Thirdly, the economic and social conditions in Russia are less developed than they are in the post-socialist countries of Central Europe. The main point here is the lack of development, the chaotic capitalism itself. Institutional insecurity and traditionalist features of mental climate are also an integral part of the picture. From the future conceptions one can read both the moral critique of present-day Russia and the realism of the remedies needed in the light of the reorganization of social life.

In a structural analysis it is fair to argue that Russian society has become proletarianized. One utopia at least has come true: the majority of the population now belongs to the proletariat. What this means is that, in the future, the Russian class structure will comprise a small and unstable elite that is in control of the power resources. There will also be a relatively small middle class with limited power resources. At the other end of the social structure, we will find a large working class with limited power resources and a growing underclass without any resources at all.

Especially in the case of working life there are many old state socialist institutions and practices that have survived in Russia. The old work culture is changing very slowly indeed. Numerous scholars have pointed out that the chief aim of managers during the transition period has been to retain their control over the factories. The reality in Russia appears to be an effort to maintain status quo.

Changes are taking place, too. At the macro level Russian society has been characterized by economic and political turbulence. Workers have experienced the same turbulence in the form of wage arrears or in decline of real wages.

Work has become increasingly intensified in Russia. All occupational groups feel that they have lost something of their former autonomy. At the same time they have to work harder than earlier. Decision-making authority is concentrated in the hands of top management, while blue-collar workers simply content themselves with following the orders of their supervisors.

The female labour force played a crucial role in building socialist societies. Today, women represent a huge potential for Russian society, but much remains to be done in order to achieve gender equality. The Russian labour markets are strictly segregated by gender. Women need support to promote female entrepreneurship, and barriers to upward mobility have to be removed.

What does the future hold for Russia in this respect? Russian working life is beginning increasingly to resemble its western counterpart. Old ideological aspects are disappearing and pure economic calculations are playing a more and more important role. The old unity of labour collectives has accordingly come under mounting pressure. Needs and interests are set to become increasingly fragmented: in this process certain groups of the working class will emerge as winners while the broad masses will lose out with the real and deep changes set to take place in the near future.

The Russian labour markets are a mixture of old traditions and practices and burgeoning new ones. The old practices are represented by network-like recruitment, where internal recruitment and personal relations play a key role.

The different labour turnover rates in the capital region and smaller towns and especially rural areas also testify to the continued presence of old obstacles to labour mobility. In relative terms the strongest position is held by those younger workers who have a good education and who work in specific branches of the private sector, such as banking and private services, excluding catering and shops. The old Soviet middle class which comprised many specialists and professionals from the state sector – teachers, nurses, accountants, scientific workers, etc. – have seen their status decline quite considerably, and their prospects for promotion or remunerating wages and interesting work are slim indeed. The argument that Russia is not a normal or typical wage worker society is confirmed by the continued problem of wage arrears in all groups of employees and in all sectors of the economy – and the very low (official or formal) level of unemployment and temporary dismissals. Indeed it can be argued that the Russian labour markets have stagnated on a general level, even though it continues to function on a differentiated level – people do change jobs and are recruited and fired, but in most cases only informally. The private sector plays a major role in the Russian economy formally, but much of the official private sector is private only artificially – the 'real' private sector is very small and has no economic significance. The unofficial part of the private sector – the so-called grey or black economy – is an entirely different case, it is economically significant and employs a very large number of people. As Sam Vakin (2000, 2) notes: 'The black economy is a cash economy. It is liquid and fast. It increases the velocity of money. It injects much-needed foreign exchange into economy and inadvertently increases money supply and the resulting money aggregates.' He goes on to argue that 'without black economy many of the economies of the transition countries would have gone bankrupt long ago.' If international estimates of the size of the informal sector as a proportion of the whole national economy (60%) are true, that would explain a significant part of people's ability to cope in a very unstable and unpredictable economy, which is virtually non-monetary by nature.

Even though large numbers of people have to rely on a wide range of different sources of income, our results suggest that such sources as second jobs or plot farming are an option only for a limited number of people, i.e. for those who have the financial and social capital (contacts and skills) to invest in these activities. For those who do not have these resources, the only options are to rely on networks of friends, relatives and neighbours or to engage themselves in petty trading. In a situation where people have to spend much of their time simply to satisfy their basic needs (e.g. food and shelter), there is not much scope for social or other forms of activity.

We argue then that this fact goes a long way towards explaining the 'miracle of patience' in Russia than do the traditions of submission to secular or divine forces. Russian people are not passive and indifferent to the problems of their everyday life and those of society. Most of them just want to lead a normal life: employment, security and services that work. It would seem that the moral order of society is in jeopardy: this is evident in the large proportion of those who agree with the statement that in order to cope in Russian society, it is necessary to break the law and be dishonest. The low levels of trust in virtually all official institutions in society also testify to the crumbling moral order. In 1998 there is only a very thin layer in society which shows even the slightest faith in the future and in the country's to leaders.

The phenomenal rise of Vladimir Putin to Russian Presidency caused some confusion among both western and Russian commentators. He was quite widely seen as a 'man without qualities' and as a first sign of a return to authoritarianism. The war in Chechnya was no doubt one of the reasons for his success in the Presidential elections, but the general disorder in the economy and in society at large played into his hands as well.

However, the future of Russia is not entirely down to Putin or even the government, which still does not enjoy very high levels of trust among the populace. It goes without saying that Russia's development into a fully-fledged capitalist society will take a great deal of time and there are numerous obstacles that have to be overcome in every sphere of society. The August crash in 1998 had beneficial impacts for domestic industrial production, and during the present year there have been encouraging signs of real growth. But continued growth and overall development does not depend economic policy or pure political decisions alone: it is crucially important that the issue of the informal institutions and civil society is taken seriously as well. As long as even the super-rich Russians do not trust their country but continue to transfer their monies to foreign banks, there is little hope of a better future. Organizations and interest groups should have a role in formulating strategies and decisions concerning the development of the country, and a state of affairs should be allowed to develop that Gorbachev saw as a precondition for the development of the Soviet Union, i.e. glasnost.

As our results have shown, the Russian people are not just 'talking heads of authoritarian ideology', but they share a broad consensus of opinion on certain issues and differ widely in their values on others. Russian people see the loss of the integrity of political and economic elites as the main cause for their miseries, even though many of them think it is also people's own fault that the economy is in ruins. Just society, for Russians, in not an egalitarian society, but a society that rewards education and hard work and that provides basic social security for all its members. In general, people want to see stability in their lives, not a superpower status or abstract freedom. They also like to see a strong and competent leader in control – but even more, they want to have a say in running the country and they want the country to be governed by law.

Bibliography

Aanason, J., *The future that failed. Origins and destinies of the Soviet model* (London: Routledge, 1993).

Ahiezer, A., *Rossia. Kritika istoricheskogo opita* (Novosibirsk: Sibirsky Kronograph 1991, 1997).

Alashev, S., 'Informal relations in the Soviet system of production', in S. Clarke (ed), *Management and Industry in Russia: Formal and informal relations in the Period of Transition* (Cheltenham: Edward Elgar, 1995).

Andreyenkova, N., 'The Development of Collective Forms of Labour Organization in the USSR', in A. Kasvio and E. Kaukonen (eds), *Working Life in Transition. Proceedings of a Finnish-Soviet Seminar* (1985), pp. 22-30, research reports no 8, Department of Sociology and Social Psychology, University of Tampere.

Arakelian, A., *Industrial Management on the USSR* (Washington: Public Affairs Press, 1950).

Ashwin, S., *Endless patience: Explaining Soviet and Post-Soviet social stability.* Communist and Post-Communist Studies 1 (1998), pp. 187-198.

Blom, R., 'Integration of a different kind', in I. Alanen (ed), *The Baltic states at a crossroads*, Publications of the Department of Sociology, University of Jyväskylä 56, 1993.

Blom, R., *The regulation and institutionalization in the Baltic states*, Research Report of the Department of Sociology and Social Psychology, University of Tampere A: 27, 1996.

Blom, R.,'Class differences in consciousness and reproduction', in M. Kivinen (ed), *Kalamari Union* (Aldershot: Ashgate, 1998).

Blom, R. (ed), *What was changed in Finland. A sociological picture of 1990's* (Helsinki: Gaudeamus, 1999).

Blom, R. et al., *Structuration of work situation in Finland and Soviet Estonia,* Research Report of the Department of Sociology and Social Psychology, University of Tampere no 16, 1989.

Blom, R., Kivinen, M., Melin, H. and Rannik, E. *The Economic System and the Work Situation: A Comparison of Finland and Estonia, International Sociology*, Vol 6, no 3 (1991), pp. 343–360.

Blom, R., Kivinen, M., Melin, H. and Rantalaiho, L. *The Scope Logic Approach to Class Analysis* (Aldershot: Avebury, 1992).

Brunetti, A., Kisunko, G. and Weder, B., *Institutions in transition. Reliability of rules and economic performance in former socialist countries,* World Bank Working Paper series, no 1809, August 1997.

Burawoy, M. and Krotov, P., *The Economic Basis of Russian Political Crisis, New Left Review* no 198 (1992), pp. 49–69.

Burawoy, M. and Krotov, P., *The Soviet transition from socialism to capitalism: Worker control and economic bargaining in the wood industry, American Sociological Review* 57 (1992), pp. 16–36.

Burawoy, M., *Two Methods in Search of Science, Scokpol versus Trotsky, Theory & Society,* Vol 18, no 6 (1989), pp. 759–805.

Burawoy, M., *The Soviet descent into capitalism, American Journal of Sociology,* 102 (1997), pp. 1430–44.

Burawoy, M., *The Politics of Production: Factory regimes under capitalism and socialism* (London: Verso, 1985).

Bäckman, J., '"New Russian" and Social Change', in M. Kivinen (ed), *The Kalamari Union* (Aldershot: Avebury, 1998).

Chernish, M., *Social mobility in the transition period, Sociologichecki Zhurnal*, #1 (1994).

Clarke, S., *Labour Market Behaviour and institutions in the transition to a market economy in Russia*, mimeo, University of Warwick, 1998.

Clarke, S., *Do Russian Households have Survival Strategies?*, www.warwick.ac.uk/fac/soc/comlabstuds/russia (1999).

Clarke, S. and Kabalina, V., *Privatisations and the Struggle for Control of the Enterprise in Russia*, paper presented at the Conference on Russia in Transition, Cambridge, 15th–16th December 1994.

Clarke, S., *Structural Adjustment without Mass Unemployment? Lessons from Russia* (Cheltenham: Edward Elgar, 1998).

Clarke, S., *Trade unions and non-payment of wages in Russia. International Journal of Manpower* 19 (1998b), pp. 68-94.

Clarke, S., *New Forms of Labour Contract and Labour Flexibility in Russia*, www.warwick.ac.uk/fac/soc/comlabstuds/russia (1999a).

Clarke, S., *Employment in the New Private Sector in Russia*, www.warwick.ac.uk/fac/soc/comlabstuds/russia (199b).

Clarke, S., *New Forms of Employment and Household Survival Strategies in Russia*, (Coventry: ISITO/CCLS, 1999c).

Clarke, S., (2000) *Contradictions and class conflict in Russia in transition*, www.warwick.ac.uk/fac/soc/comlabstuds/russia (2000).

Clarke, S. (ed), *Conflict and Change in the Russian Industrial Enterprise* (Cheltenham: Edward Elgar, 1996).

Clarke, S., Fairbrother, P., Burawoy, M., and Krotov, P., *What about workers?* (London: Verso, 1993).

Clarke, S., Kabalina, V., *The Restructuring of employment and formation of labour market in Russia*, Working Paper 13 (Warwick, Moscow: CCLS & ISITO, 1996).

Commander, S., Tolstopiatenko, A. and Yemtsov, R., *Channels of redistribution: Inequality and poverty in the Russian transition*, Working Paper number 42, The William Davidson Institute at the University of Michigan Business School, 1997.

DeWitt, N., *Education and Professional Employment in the USSR* (London: Bodley Head, 1961).

Djilas, M. *Uusi luokka – kommunismin todelliset kasvot* (Jyväskylä: Gummerus, 1975). [The New Class]

Dunford, M.F., 'Differential development, institutions, modes of regulation and comparative transitions to capitalism. Russia, the Commonwealth of Independent States and former German Democratic Republic', in M.F. Dunford, *Capital, the State and Regional Development*, Studies in Society and Space (Pion Ltd, 1998).

Eskov, G., *Ukreplenie politicheskoi osnovi sovetskogo gosudarstva* (1983).

Eyal, G., Szelenyi, I. and Townsley, E., *A theory of post-communist managerialism. New Left Review* 222 (1997), pp. 60–92.

Featherman, D., *Opportunity and change* (Hancover, 1982).

Gerber, T. and Hout, M., *More shock than therapy: Market transition, employment, and income in Russia, 1991-1995, American Journal of Sociology* 1 (1998), pp. 1–50.

Gimpelson, V., *The labour market and social re-ranking in countries under transition. Seven transition countries compared*, paper presented for the conference 'Economic Sociology at the Edge of 3rd Millennium', 14–15 January 2000, Moscow.

Gordon, L.A. and Nazimova, A., 'The Socio-occupational Structure of the Soviet Working Class', in Yanowitch (ed), *Social Structure of the USSR. Recent Soviet Studies* (New York: M.E. Sharpe, 1986).

Gosudarstvo i sotsialnaya stratififikatsia sovetskogo i postsovetskogo obschestv. Syktivkar. (1996), p. 53.

Gowan, P., *Neo-Liberal Theory and practice for Eastern Europe, New Left Review*, 213 (1995).

Gowan, P., *Eastern Europe, western power and neo-liberalism, New Left Review*, 216 (1996).

Grosfield, I. et al., *Dynamism and Inertia on the Russian Labour Market: A Model of Segmentation*, Working Paper no 246, April, William Davidson Institute, 1999.

Hannah, A., *Totalitarianism* (San Diego: Harvest Books, 1968).

Ilyin, V., 'Social Contradictions and Conflicts in State Enterprises in the Transition Period', in Clarke (ed), *Conflict and Change in the Russian Industrial Enterprise*, pp. 32–64.

Karppinen, A., *Venäjän aatetta jäljittämässä* (Helsinki: WSOY, 1999).

Kennedy, M. and Suny, R. (eds), *Intellectuals and the Articulation of the Nation* (University of Michigan Press, 1999).

Kivinen, M., (1998) *Sosiologia ja Venäjä* (Helsinki: Hanki ja Jää, 1998). [Sociology and Russia]

Kivinen, M., *Sociology in Russia* (Helsinki: Alexanteri Institute, 2000).

Kolodko, G.W., *Ten Years of Post-Socialist Transition: Lessons for Policy Reforms,* Policy Research Working Papers no 2905, World Bank, April, 1990.

Kornai, J., *Vision and Reality, Market and State* (New York: Harvester Wheatsheaf, 1990).

Kuorsalo, A. et al., *Venäjän rosvokapitalismin haaksirikko* (Helsinki: Edita, 1999).

Lane, C., *The impact of the Economic and Political System on Social Stratification and Social Mobility, Soviet Lower White-Collar Workers in Comparative Perspective. Sociology,* Vol 21, no 2 (1987), pp. 171–188.

Lane, D., *Soviet Economy and Society* (Oxford: Basil Blackwell, 1985).

Ledeneva, A., *Russia's economy of favours. Blat, networking and informal exchange* (Cambridge: Cambridge University Press, 1998).

Linz, S., *Red Executives: Are They Winners or Losers in Russia's Economic Reforms?,* Working Paper Number 66, The William Davidson Institute at the University of Michigan Business School, 1997.

Lipset, S. and Bendix, R., *Social mobility in industrial society* (University of California Press, 1967).

Littler, G., 'Soviet-type Societies and Labour Process', in Thompson (ed), *Work, Employment and Unemployment* (Philadelphia: Open University Press, 1984).

Lloyd, J., *Eastern deformers and neo-marxist revieweers, New Left Review* 216 (1964).

Lockwood, D., 'Social integration and system integration', in Zollschan and Hirsch (eds), *Explorations of social change* (London: Routledge, 1964).

Melin, H., *Work situation of main occupational groups revisited*, Baltic-Nordic Project, Working papers 1, 1995. Department of Sociology and Social Psychology, University of Tampere.

Melin, H., *Suunnitelman varjossa. Tutkimus yritysjohtajista Neuvostoliitossa ja Venäjällä*, Acta Universitatis Tamperensis, ser A, Vol 489, 1996. [In the Shadow of the Plan, Factory Directors in the USSR and Russia]

Melin, H., (1998) 'Suomen luokkarakenne', in Saksala (ed), *Muutoksen sosiologia* (Helsinki: YLE, 1998). [Finnish Class Structure]

Mellor, R., *Changing cities in Post-Soviet Russia. New Left Review* 236 (1999), pp. 53–76.

Mouzelis, M., *Back to sociological theory. Constitution of social orders* (London: Macmillan, 1991).

Muller, K., *Modernizing Eastern Europe: Theoretical Problems and Political Dilemmas*, Archives Européennes de Sociologie. Vol XXXIII, no 1 (1992).

Nee, V., *A theory of market transition: From redistribution to markets in state socialism, American Sociological Review* 54 (1989), pp. 663–81.

Nee, V., *Social inequalities in reforming state socialism: Between redistribution and markets in China. American Sociological Review* 55 (1991), pp. 663–81.

Nee, V., *The emergence of market society: Changing mechanisms of stratification in China, American Journal of Sociology* 101 (1996), pp. 908–49.

Nee, V. and Matthews, R., *Market transition and societal transformation in reforming state socialism, Annual Review of Sociology* 22 (1996), pp. 401–35.

Nikula, J. *From State-Dependency to Genuine Worker Movement? The Working Class in Socialism and Post-Socialism* (Tampere: University of Tampere, 1997).

Nowe, A., *The Soviet Economic System* (London: Allen & Unwin, 1977).

Pakulski, J., *The Dying of class or of Marxist class theory? International Sociology*, Vol 8, no 3 (1993).

Puffer, S., (1996) 'A Portrait of Russian Business Leaders', in Puffer, S. (ed), *Business and Management in Russia,* pp. 17–33 (Cheltenham: Edward Elgar, 1996).

Raiser, M., *Trust in Transition*, ERDB Working Papers, no 39, 1999.

Rose, D., *Between state and market*, Studies in Public Policy 196 (Glasgow: University of Strathlyde, 1991).

Rukavishnikov, S., (1999): *Is Russia Really becoming a Thrid World country? Unemployment Risks in the time of post-soviet restructuring*, William Davidson Institute, Working Papers no 28, 1999.

Russia Survey, The Economist, 12 July 1997.

Rutkevich, M., *Toward Social Homogeneity* (Moscow: Progress Publishers, 1984).

Simagin, Yu, *Ob otsenkakh massthabov dopolnitelnoi zanyatosti naseleniya. Voprosi ekonomiki* 1 (1998), pp. 99–104.

Simon, R., *Russia's Crises. Capital & Class*, no 68 (1999), pp. 1–7.

Skidelsky, R., *The world after communism* (London: Macmillan, 1995).

Slapentokh, V., *Russian patience: a reasonable behaviour and a social strategy, European Journal of Sociology* 2 (1995), pp. 247-80.

Social distinctions in modern Russia, sample and field condition report, Institute of Sociology, Russian Academy of Sciences, Moscow 1999.

Soloviev, E., 'Pravovoi nihilism i gumanisticheskii smisl prava', in *Kvintessentia* (Politizdat, 1990).

Sorokin, P., *Chelovek, tsivilizatsia, obshestvo* (Politizdat, 1992).

Southworth, C., *The Making of the Russian Working Class: Workplace Conflicts and Economic Development in Post-Soviet Factories of the Urals*, www.sscnet.ucla.edu/soc/groups/ccsa/southworth.htm (1999).

Srubar, I., *War der reale Sozialismus modern? Versuch einer strukturellen Bestimmung, Kolner Zeitschrift für Soziologie und Sozialpsychologie*, Vol 43, no 3 (1991).

Srubar, I., *Variants of the Transformation Process in Central Europe. A Comparative Assessment, Zeitschrift für Soziologie* 23(3), (1994).

SSSR. *Izdatelstvo 'Sovetskaya entsiklopedia'* (1977).

Sutela, P., *The Road to Russian Market Economy* (Helsinki: Kikimora Publications, 1998).

Sutela, P., *The lure of the authorian temptation*, Bank of Finland, Institute for Economies of Transition, Russian Economy, The Month in Review 7 July 2000.

Szelenyi, I. and Kondrad, G., *Intellectuals on the road to class power* (New York, 1978).

Sztompka, P., *Civilizational Incompetence: The trap of Post-Communist Societies. Zeitschrift für Soziologie* 22, 2 (1993).

Tong, Y., *Mass alienation under state socialism and after, Communist and Post-Communist Studies* 2 (1995), pp. 215–37.
Tsipko, A., 'Istoki stalinisma', in *Nauka i zhizn* (1988, N 11,12, 1988, N 1,2).
Unicef, *Women in Transition – a Summary*, Regional Monitoring Project No 6, Florence 1999.
Wesolowski, W., (1969) 'The Notions of Strata and Class in Socialist Society', in Beteille (ed), *Social Inequality*, pp. 122–45 (Suffolk: Penguin Books, 1969).
Wright, E., *Classes* (London: Verso, 1985).
Wright, E.O., *Class, Crisis and the State* (London: New Left Books, 1978).
Wright, E.O. (1997) *Class Counts* (Cambridge: University of Cambridge Press, 1997).
www.cspp.strath.ac.uk
www.russiatoday.com/features.
www.stat.fi/tilastot/suomi
Zaslavskaya, T., *Social Structure of Russian Society today, Social Sciences* Vol XXVIII, no 3 (1997), pp. 6–27.

Index